MARK WILSON'S GREATEST

INSTANT MAGIC TRICKS

More Than Fifty Amazing Illusions
You Can Perform Anywhere

An imprint of Running Press
Philadelphia • London

ACKNOWLEDGMENTS

The contents of this book do not represent the efforts of only two, three, or a dozen individuals; rather, they represent all those magicians of the past and the present who have labored so diligently to create, perfect, and present the Art of Magic.

Just as a stalagmite, buried unseen in a dark cave, builds from tiny drops into a towering structure, so has our Art increased through the centuries, shrouded in a like darkness of secrecy which remains a prerequisite to its growth.

With this book, you will join the ranks of those who have learned these inner secrets—and you must acknowledge and respect those whose contributions we enjoy. *Acknowledge* by being aware of the countless hours of study, work, and practice that have been expended by the magicians of the past to create our Art. *Respect* the magicians of today by never revealing any of these hard-earned secrets.

This, then, is the grateful acknowledgment of this book: *to the Magicians of all times and places,* for their countless contributions to the Art of Magic.

© 1995, 1988, 1981, 1975 Greg Wilson

Published and produced by arrangement with Ottenheimer Publishers, Inc. All rights reserved under the Pan-American and International Copyright Conventions. This book may not be reproduced in whole or in part, in any form or by any means, electronic or mechanical, including photocopying, recording, or by any information storage and retrieval system now known or hereafter invented, without written permission from the publisher.

9 8 7 6 5 4 3 2 1
Digit on the right indicates the number of this printing.

OPI MA023A

Printed in Hong Kong

Library of Congress Cataloging-in-Publication Number 94-73873

ISBN 1-56138-468-2

Jacket design by Toby Schmidt
Front cover photography by Weaver Lilley
Interior design by Ruthie Thompson
Compiled by Caroline Schweiter
Edited by Liz Kaufman

Published by Courage Books, an imprint of Running Press Book Publishers
125 South Twenty-second Street
Philadelphia, Pennsylvania 19103-4399

TABLE OF CONTENTS

ABOUT THE AUTHOR...
MARK WILSON

Mark Wilson has performed magic for more people than any other magician in the 3,500-year history of the art. During his successful career over the past 30 years, Mark Wilson has shared his wondrous magic with the world in many ways:

♦ Starred in the first weekly network magic series, *Magic Land of Allakazam*, which aired for two years on CBS, and for three years on ABC networks; six *Magic Circus* specials; *Magic of Mark Wilson* syndicated series; four *HBO Magic Specials*; *Magic of China, Children of China, Mr. Magic* syndicated specials; and many more.

♦ Developed international programming, including television specials for the NHK, NTV, and ASAHI Japanese networks and for Korea, Canada, Hong Kong, Australia, Great Britain, and People's Republic of China. Wilson's U.S. productions have aired throughout South America, Europe, Southeast Asia, Pacific Rim countries, and elsewhere.

♦ Authored *Mark Wilson's Complete Course in Magic*, the most popular book of magic instruction in history, with over 300,000 copies published.

♦ Served as creative consultant and supplier of magic to countless television series, such as *Columbo, Simon and Simon, Love Boat, Circus of the Stars, Perfect Strangers, Dear John,* and *The Odd Couple*.

♦ Instructs Hollywood's top stars in the performance of magic. Past and present celebrity students include Cary Grant, Tony Curtis, Peter Falk, Bill Bixby, Jackie Gleason, Cher, Johnny Carson, Burt Reynolds, and many others.

♦ Prepares entertainment packages for many of the world's finest theme parks, world's fairs, expositions, and major corporations worldwide.

♦ Most notably, in 1980 Mark Wilson was the first foreign magician to perform on mainland China since the founding of the People's Republic of China. He is the world's most honored magician, with *two* prestigious "Magician of the Year" awards and the "Master's Fellowship" from the Academy of Magical Arts. He has also won the "Superstar of Magic," "Magician of the Decade," and "Lifetime Achievement" awards.

INTRODUCTION

Welcome to a very special branch of the magical arts—Instant Magic. Instant Magic refers to tricks and puzzles that can be performed with objects carried in your pockets or found in any home or office. In other words, the tricks in this book will allow you to perform magic practically anywhere, at any time, on the spur of the moment.

In some cases, you may have to do a little advance preparation before performing. However, once the setup is complete, you're ready to go. Other tricks can be done with common, everyday objects, such as coins and playing cards. In some cases, these items can even be borrowed from spectators.

As you learn the tricks in this book, try to arrange them in an entertaining sequence. This is what magicians call "routining." In other words, instead of doing a hodgepodge of tricks, try performing two or three card tricks in a row. Do the same with tricks using ropes, money, etc. The goal is to achieve a smooth, logical progression of tricks that blend into one another.

There are no hard and fast rules regarding which tricks should be routined with other tricks. That's what makes magic fun! You can experiment and develop routines with tricks that you enjoy the most and that best fit your personality and performing style.

The tricks in this book are very versatile, because most of them can be done for one person or for a small group. Therefore, you can entertain almost anywhere—at home, the office, picnics, even in the car or on an airplane.

Like every other type of magic, it is important that you practice each and every trick thoroughly before performing. There's nothing worse than a magician who blunders a trick due to insufficient practice. When you can perform your magic smoothly, effortlessly, and without hesitation, you are ready!

If you'd like to learn more about magic and take the next step in exploring our wonderful art, please write to me.

Happy Magic!

Mark Wilson

Mark Wilson
c/o Magic International
P.O. Box 801839
Santa Clarita, CA 91380-1839

CHAPTER 1

IMPROMPTU MAGIC

Here are some "quick tricks" that you can do anywhere at any time. Some are puzzles rather than tricks, others are more in the nature of stunts, but the majority are quite deceptive and will arouse interest among people who see them. In fact, that is the great purpose of this branch of magic; for once you have gained people's interest with something trivial and find that they want to see more, you can go into your regular routine with confidence since you know you already have a receptive audience.

These impromptu tricks are sometimes termed "ice-breakers" because when people seem cold or aloof, particularly at a party where very few know one another, they will often "thaw" quite rapidly when you show them a few bafflers. Also, some of these tricks, particularly the puzzle type, are expendable, in the sense that as a part of the presentation you can explain them to your audience, and they can use them to puzzle their friends as well.

At the same time, never explain any of the real "magic" bafflers. Keep these impromptu effects for yourself—because, as you advance in magic, you will find that some of the keenest spectators, when describing later what you did, are apt to magnify trifling perplexities into near-miracles. When that happens it is up to you, as a magician, to turn it to your own advantage.

JUMPING RUBBER BAND

EFFECT

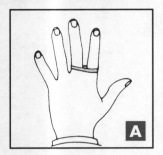

NOTE: A, B, and C show the spectators' viewpoint. In all the illustrations, the fingers are pointing up.

A You place a rubber band around your first and second fingers.

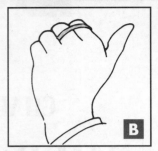

B You close your hand into a fist.

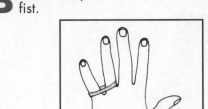

C When you open your hand, the band magically jumps to your third and fourth fingers.

METHOD

All method illustrations are from the magician's viewpoint.

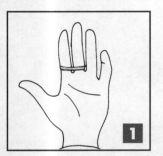

1 Place the rubber band around the bases of your first and second fingers on your left hand. If the band is too loose, you may put it around twice. Experiment with whatever rubber band you're using, so that you get the proper tension on the band. Your hand is toward the spectators, and your palm faces you.

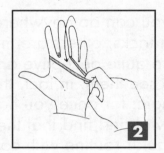

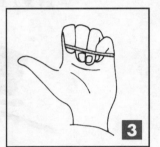

2 Close your left hand into a fist, by bending your fingers into your palm. At the same time, secretly use the first finger of your right hand to stretch the rubber band so that the tips of all four left fingers can be inserted into the rubber band.

3 This is how your hand now looks to you. (To the spectators, your hand will appear as in B.)

4 Straighten out your fingers and the band will automatically jump to a new position around your left third and fourth fingers.

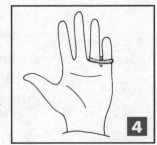

REVERSE JUMPING RUBBER BAND

EFFECT

You make the rubber band jump back from your third and fourth fingers to your first and second fingers.

METHOD

1 Simply reverse the procedure used for the first jump.

2 After the band has jumped to your third and fourth fingers, fold your hand into a fist again. As you do, use the first finger of your right hand to stretch the rubber band.

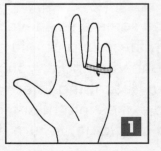

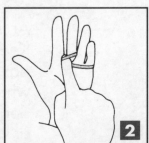

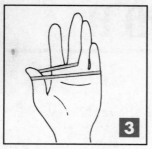

3 Another way is to use your left thumb to stretch the band.

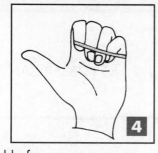

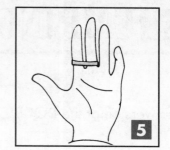

5 When you straighten out your fingers, the band will jump back to your first and second fingers.

4 Then, when you close your left hand, secretly insert the tips of all four left fingers, as you did before.

DOUBLE JUMPING RUBBER BAND I

EFFECT

You can double the mystery of this trick by magically making two rubber bands change places.

METHOD

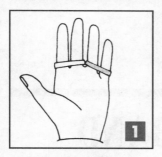

1 Place one rubber band (a white one, for instance) around your left first and second fingers. Place a second, different-colored rubber band (say a blue one) around your left third and fourth fingers.

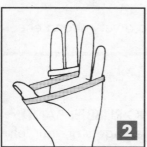

2 Before you close your hand into a fist, reach over with your left thumb and stretch the rubber band that is around the third and fourth fingers, as shown.

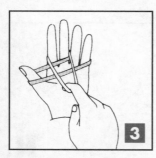

4 Secretly place the tips of all four fingers into both rubber bands as you close your hand. The fingers of the left hand go into the opening indicated by the arrow.

5 At the same time that you insert the fingers of the left hand into the bands, release both the bands from your left thumb and from the first finger on the right hand. Your hand will look like this to you.

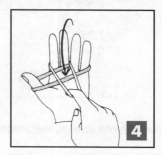

6 Call the spectators' attention to the fact that the white band is around your first and second fingers, and the blue band is around your third and fourth fingers. To the spectators, it looks like this.

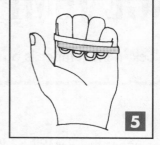

3 Use your right first finger to pull the band that is around the first and second fingers of your left hand, as shown.

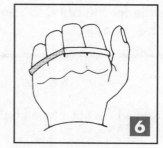

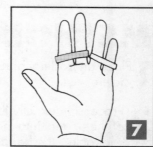

7 Just straighten out your fingers. The bands will jump to the opposite fingers.

DOUBLE JUMPING RUBBER BAND II

EFFECT

The effect is the same as in the first version of the DOUBLE JUMPING RUBBER BAND described above; however, the method is slightly different.

METHOD

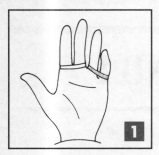

1 Place the two rubber bands on your fingers, as before.

2 With the first finger of the right hand, secretly stretch, or "nip," each of the bands away from the left hand.

3 Insert the second finger of the right hand into the loops

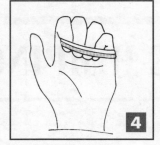

formed by the right first finger and spread the loops open, using both right fingers.

4 Fold your left hand into a fist and insert the tips of the left fingers into the opening formed by the right fingers. To you, your hand looks like this.

5 Straighten out your fingers in the usual way, and the bands will change places.

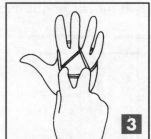

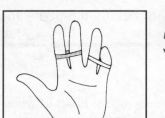

CHALLENGE JUMPING RUBBER BAND

The addition of an extra band to lock in the jumper is a clever touch that turns a simple trick into a very strong effect.

EFFECT

This can be used as a follow-up for either the JUMPING RUBBER BAND or the DOUBLE JUMPING RUBBER BAND. You explain that to make it impossible for the band to jump, you will encircle the tips of all of the fingers of your left hand individually with another rubber band.

METHOD

1 Place an additional rubber band around the tips of the fingers of your left hand, as shown in the picture.

2 Proceed in exactly the same way as you did before. Fold your hand into a fist and insert the tips of the fingers into the band that is to jump. Straighten out your fingers, and behold—another minor miracle—the band jumped just as before!

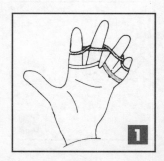

LINKING PAPER CLIPS

This is a most entertaining combination magic trick and puzzle. After you perform it, everyone will want to try it. If someone should figure it out, don't worry—they'll have as much fun with it as you do.

EFFECT

You show two paper clips and a dollar bill. You give the bill a three-way fold and use the clips to fasten the folds in place. As you pull the ends of the pleated bill, slowly but steadily the clips come closer together. You finish the pull with a sharp snap, as the clips fly from the bill and land on the table, linked together!

METHOD

The trick is almost automatic. It depends entirely upon the proper placement of the clips. Practice the setup until you can place the clips in position quickly and neatly, so observers will be unable to follow and will therefore find it difficult to duplicate the trick.

1 Start by holding the bill open between both of your hands.

2 Fold ⅓ of the length of the bill over to the right, as shown.

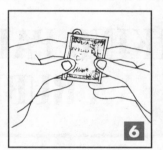

3 Place one of the paper clips over this fold to hold it in place, and push it down so it is snug against the top edge of the bill.

4 The clip should be positioned near the end of the folded portion of the bill, directly over the number that shows its value.

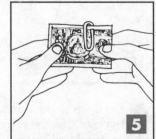

5 Turn the bill completely around so that you are looking at the other side. Do not turn the bill upside down in the process; the clip should still be at the top, as shown.

6 Fold the left end of the bill over to the right, as shown in the illustration.

7 Put the other paper clip on the bill from the top, thus holding this end in place too. Clip together just the two front folds—those that are toward you.

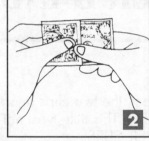

8 The clip should be positioned near the end of the bill over its number value, as shown here.

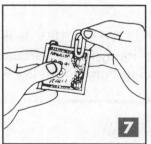

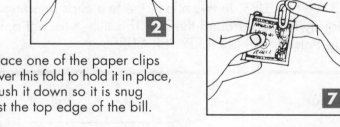

9 If both clips have been properly placed, the bill should look as shown in this view.

10 Firmly grip both ends of the bill near the top and start to pull them apart. As the bill unfolds, the clips will start moving together, still pinned to the bill.

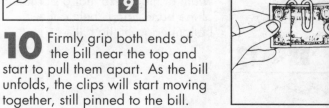

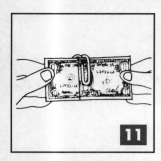

11 When you reach the point where the clips are practically on top of each other, give the ends of the bill a sharp tug.

12 The bill will open out and send the paper clips sailing across the table, linking them as they go!

COMMENTS AND SUGGESTIONS

The trick is particularly effective with jumbo clips that are longer and wider, so the linking can be followed easily. With ordinary paper clips, only a slight tug is needed; otherwise they may fly clear across the table as they link. If they go off the edge, the effect will be weakened.

With practice, placing the clips in position becomes a simple and rapid process. If using small clips, you can put two on the top edge and another pair on the bottom edge. The tug will shoot them in opposite directions, and each pair will be found linked.

LINKING PAPER CLIPS WITH A RUBBER BAND

EFFECT

Here is a clever addition to LINKING PAPER CLIPS. In this effect, the two clips mysteriously link themselves and also link to a rubber band that was previously looped around the bill. This little twist not only takes the effect one step further, it also creates a very puzzling finish for LINKING PAPER CLIPS.

METHOD

1 Follow Steps 1 through 4 as described in LINKING PAPER CLIPS, placing the first clip over the folded portion of the bill, as shown.

2 Loop a rubber band of the size shown around the right end of the bill. The rubber band should be slightly longer than the width of the bill so that a portion of the band hangs below the bottom edge of the bill.

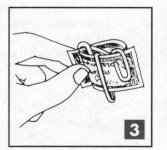

3 Fold back the right end of the bill and attach the second paper clip, as you did in the original routine. If both clips and the rubber band have been properly placed, the bill should look like this.

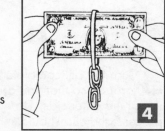

4 Firmly grip both ends of the bill and pull them apart. The rubber band will remain looped around the bill with the paper clips linked to it in a chain, as shown.

COMMENTS AND SUGGESTIONS

It is a good idea to practice this a few times until you understand why it works as it does. Once you understand the way it works, concentrate on placing the paper clips and the rubber band in exactly the same position every time you perform the trick. You can then succeed in baffling spectators without fear of making a mistake in the handling of the props.

JUMPING MATCH

EFFECT

During a casual encounter with a group of friends, you announce that you have discovered a surefire method of checking your own pulse. After removing two ordinary, wooden kitchen matches from your pocket, you place one across the palm of your left hand. You explain that this match will serve as the counter. The second match is slipped under the first. For this demonstration, it will serve as the transmitter. As the spectators watch the counter, it is seen to bounce rhythmically as if counting out your heartbeats. Suddenly it stops, then beats erratically, creating a humorous finish to this puzzling feat. The spectators are handed the matches for examination and are challenged to try to duplicate the test. Of course they can't, and the two matches will keep them busy for days in vain attempts to make the experiment work.

SECRET AND PREPARATION

Use large, wooden kitchen matches for this effect. They are not prepared in any way; therefore, they can be borrowed. The secret to this experiment lies in your unseen manipulation of the transmitter match.

METHOD

1 Place the first, or counter, match across your left palm, as shown. Position the end of this match so that it is resting against the side of your first finger with the head of the match pointed toward you.

2 The second, or transmitter, match is held between the thumb and first finger of your right hand. Your second finger presses its nail against the back of the match, as shown.

3 If you exert pressure against the match with the nail of the second finger, and slowly and imperceptibly slide the match across the nail, the match will create the necessary unseen pulses.

4 Position the transmitter match under the counter match, as shown. Secretly slide your right second fingernail across the match as described in Step 3. The right-hand transmitter match will cause the left-hand counter match to jump in a rhythmic beat.

COMMENTS AND SUGGESTIONS

This fine pocket trick is completely impromptu and can be very mystifying, if done well. Large, wooden kitchen matches are best since they show up better and make the secret move easier to perform. Remember that the counter match won't jump unless your right second fingernail is pressing firmly against its match when you slide it across. Another patter theme for this effect is to explain that you have learned how to magically magnetize matches. Rub the first (transmitter) match several times on your sleeve or the tablecloth. Sure enough, when you hold the magnetized first match up against the second (counter) match, it vibrates and shakes as if it really were impelled by some strange, new power!

FLYING MATCH

EFFECT

You show an ordinary book of paper matches. The book is opened, and the matches, all still attached to the book, are counted for all to see. One match is removed from the book, and the matchbook cover is closed. You light the match, by striking it on the book, and then blow the match out. You make the burnt match vanish as you throw it toward the matchbook. When the matchbook is opened by a spectator, the burnt match is found inside, attached to the matchbook like the rest of the matches! As an added "convincer," the matches are counted, and the number is found to be the same as at the start of the effect.

SECRET AND PREPARATION

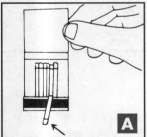

A Before you perform this clever trick, you open the matchbook and bend one match in the first row down at the base, as shown.

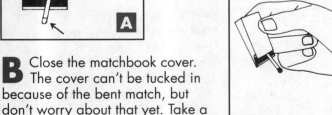

B Close the matchbook cover. The cover can't be tucked in because of the bent match, but don't worry about that yet. Take a second, loose match, strike it, and set the head of the bent match on fire. Quickly blow out both matches.

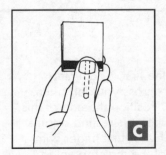

C Now you must hide the burnt match that is still attached to the book. Place your left thumb on top of the matchbook so that it completely covers the bent match. The illustration shows how to conceal the match with your left thumb and hold the matchbook closed at the same time. With this secret preparation completed, you are ready to perform.

METHOD

1 With the bent match concealed by your left thumb, open the cover to the matchbook with your right hand, and ask a spectator to watch closely as you count the matches in the book. Be sure to keep the bent match hidden, and don't let the spectator take the matchbook from you as you count. Just hold the matchbook so that it's easy for the spectator to see the matches, then bend each match slightly forward with your right fingers as you count them.

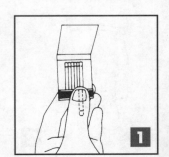

NOTE: It is best to have only ten to twelve matches remaining in the book when you perform this trick. This means there are fewer matches for you to count, and there is less of a chance that the spectator will see the bent match during the counting. In addition, the smaller number of matches makes the reappearance of the burnt match even more startling.

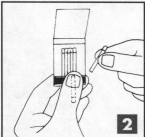

2 With your right fingers, remove one match from the first row. This must be a match that is located next to the hidden bent match. Put this match on the table and close the matchbook cover.

3 As you close the cover, hold the book up in front of you so that the back of the book is toward the spectators.

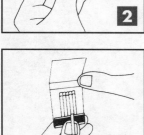

4 As your right fingers close the cover, your left thumb is under the bent match and pushes it upward into the matchbook.

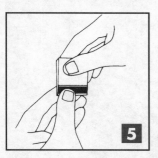

5 Immediately close the matchbook and tuck in the cover. The entire sequence takes only a few seconds and is hidden from the spectators, who see only the back of the matchbook.

6 Pick up the match you placed on the table (the one you just removed) and strike it on the matchbook. Let only the head of the match burn and then blow it out. Put the matchbook near the center of the table. Now for the magic!

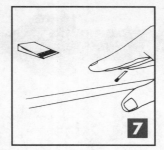

7 Pretend to pick up the match on the table with your right hand. Your right fingers really only cover the match. You slide your right hand back toward yourself.

8 As you do this, the match is secretly swept off the table and falls into your lap.

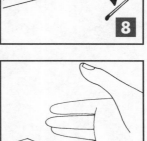

9 Hold up your right fingers, as if they contain the match. Done correctly, the illusion of picking up the match is perfect.

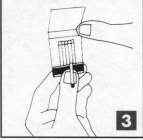

10 Apparently throw the burnt match (from your really empty hand) toward the closed matchbook. Show that your right hand is empty.

11 Have the spectator pick up the matchbook and open it. Inside the spectator will find what appears to be the original match, now burnt and firmly attached to the matchbook.

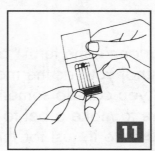

12 As a final "convincer," have the spectator count the matches. The spectator will find the number of matches to be the same as at the start of the trick!

COMMENTS AND SUGGESTIONS

The vanish of the match, its reappearance in the matchbook, and the fact that the match is burnt and attached to the matchbook—all add up to an outstanding close-up mystery.

CHAPTER 2

BETCHAS

In magical parlance, the term "betcha" is short for "I'll bet you!"—which means that you, as the magician, would be willing to bet a spectator that you can do something that they can't. Of course, you don't have to make a bet to prove your point. You can go right ahead and do it, just for the fun of it. People appreciate that because, if they have a good time watching magic, they will want to see more.

Actually, a Betcha is more of a puzzle than a trick. Betchas, however, can prove both useful and effective, so it is wise to have them available. Practically every Betcha has some neat twist that gives it audience appeal; and some, if done smoothly and fairly rapidly, may even become tricks in their own right. Although you show the audience exactly what is done, the moves may be too complex for them to follow. So instead of learning "how it's done," they only become all the more puzzled.

The best plan is to "warm up" with a few Betchas—getting people to try some trifling tricks for themselves, which will put them in a mood to appreciate the *real* magic that you show them later.

IMPOSSIBLE PENETRATION

EFFECT

You display two rolled-up dollar bills. You place a bill in the crook of each of your thumbs, one bill in each hand. By grasping the ends of the bills with the thumbs and second fingers of the opposite hands, you are able to separate your hands, causing the bills to apparently pass magically through one another. The real mystery is that the spectators are unable to duplicate the feat.

METHOD

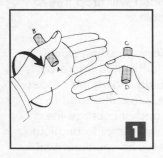

1 Roll two dollar bills into tight cylinders and hold the bills in the crooks of your thumbs, as shown.

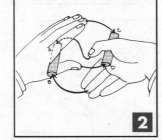

2 Rotate your hands in opposite directions, so that you can take the left-hand bill with the right thumb at A and the right second finger at B. At the same time, your left hand grasps the right-hand bill with the left thumb at D and the left second finger at C.

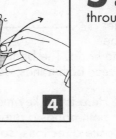

3 Held correctly, your hands should look like this. To the spectators, the illusion of the linking of your fingers and the bills is perfect.

4 Rotate your hands in opposite directions, as you pull your hands apart.

5 The bills will free themselves and appear to magically pass through each other.

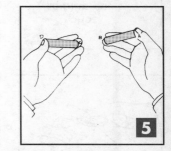

COMMENTS AND SUGGESTIONS

This effect can also be done with two corks, short pencils, or any small objects of the correct shape and size. Whatever you use, it's a very deceptive quickie. It may also be done as a puzzle. In this case, you repeat the trick over and over as the spectators try to duplicate it. Each time, do the penetration a little slower. Finally, someone will get it and start to fool the other participants. Present it this way at the next party you attend and see how much fun you will have!

RUBBER BAND RELEASE

Here is a stunt that you can perform quite easily, yet no one else is able to duplicate it.

EFFECT

You display an ordinary rubber band, twirling it between the first fingers of each hand. You proceed to touch the tips of your right thumb and first finger to the tips of your left thumb and first finger. Even though the tips of your fingers remain touching, the rubber band instantly drops to the table. Yet, when the spectator tries to duplicate the stunt, the rubber band remains trapped between the thumbs and forefingers. No matter how many times you repeat the feat, no one else is able to perform it.

METHOD

1 Begin by displaying the rubber band looped over the tips of your two first fingers, as shown.

2 Rotate your fingers around each other, as shown by the arrows, keeping the rubber band lightly stretched between your fingers.

3 Stop twirling the band and move both thumbs so that they touch the tips of the first fingers of the

Fingers and thumbs touch

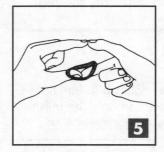
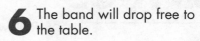

same hand. The band is now held between both hands, as shown.

4 Here is the key move. Rotate both hands a quarter turn in opposite directions, so that you are able to touch the tip of your left first finger to your right thumb and the tip of your right first finger to your left thumb, as shown. As you do this, continue to hold the tips of the fingers of each hand together, as shown in Step 3.

NOTE: This quarter-turn move, as you continue to hold the band between your fingers, is the whole secret of the mystery. Later, when the spectators try to duplicate your moves, they will neglect to hold the fingers and thumbs of each hand together and to execute the quarter turn. They will probably just touch both thumbs together and both first fingers together instead. Or, even if they touch the first fingers of each hand with the thumbs of the other hand, the trick is still impossible unless they hold the band in place, as shown in Step 4.

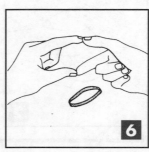

5 To release the band, spread your thumbs and first fingers apart, as shown.

6 The band will drop free to the table.

7 This very puzzling stunt is quite difficult to figure out without being shown the proper procedure. Give the band to a spectator and encourage the spectator to attempt to duplicate your moves. The spectator will most surely be unable to do so, because the spectator will fail to touch the proper fingers together and make the correct moves in order to release the band from the fingers.

COMMENTS AND SUGGESTIONS

Experiment with the rubber band until you fully understand the release positions of the fingers. When you can perform the routine smoothly and without hesitation, you will be ready to present the stunt. This deceptive little maneuver will cause a stir among your friends and keep them busy for some time.

IMPOSSIBLE KNOT

Tricks of the "Do As I Do" type are always effective, and this is one of the best. All you need are two ropes, each about 3' in length; one is for yourself, the other for a spectator. With a little practice and one simple, secret move, you can baffle spectators time after time—to the point where they will actually fool themselves!

EFFECT

You hold a length of rope with one end in each hand, and you invite a spectator to do the same with another piece of rope. Stating that it would be impossible to tie a knot in a rope without letting go of at least one end, you proceed to drape the rope over your arms, forming a series of simple loops and twists. This is done slowly, without letting go of the ends, so the spectator can copy every move you make with the rope. Still holding both ends, you shake the rope from your arms, and a knot magically appears in the center. No knot is found in the spectator's rope, even though everyone is sure the spectator has copied your every move exactly.

METHOD

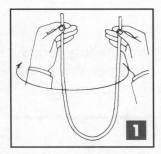

1 Hold the rope near the ends between the thumb and first finger of each hand with the rope hanging below, as shown.

2 Bring your right hand inward (toward you) and drape the rope over your left wrist, as shown.

3 Draw the right end of the rope downward and beneath the hanging loops. This divides the hanging loop into two sections, left and right.

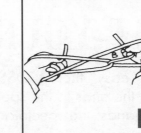

4 Insert your right hand (still holding the right end) through the left section of the loop; and, in the same continuous action, bring your hand back through the right section of the loop, nipping the rope at point A, as shown.

5 Without releasing either hand, move your right hand back to the right, bringing the nipped rope with it. Point A is now resting on the back of your right wrist.

NOTE: This is the only part of this excellent magical puzzle that is difficult to illustrate. Just try it with the rope in your hands, until you hold the rope as shown in Step 5. Another way to describe Step 4 is that your right hand, still holding its end, goes into the loop and picks up point A on the back of your right wrist. Point A is then pulled out through the loop to form the setup shown in Step 5.

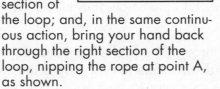

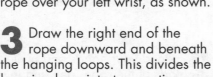

6 Move your right hand level with your left and pull the rope taut so it forms the crisscross pattern between your wrists, as shown. Note that in the illustration a new spot is indicated on the rope, point B. Point B is just below the end held by your right hand. Relax the tension on the rope and tilt both hands forward and downward, so the outside loops, which are pressed against your wrists, begin to slide over the tops of your hands.

7 You are now ready for the secret move. As the rope begins to fall off your wrists, your right hand prepares to secretly release its end and grasp the rope at point B, as described in Step 8.

8 As the loops slide completely over and off your hand, draw your hands apart. At the same time, release the right end of the rope with your thumb and first finger, and secretly grasp point B with your other three fingers. Because of the tossing movement of the loops as they fall off your wrists, the spectators are completely unaware of this small move that is the whole secret of the trick.

9 As you draw your hands apart, the right end of the rope will automatically pull through the little loops, forming a knot in the center of the rope.

10 Your right thumb and first finger immediately regain their original grip on the end of the rope, so all looks the same as the knot is formed.

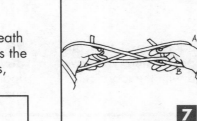

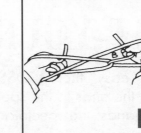

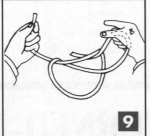

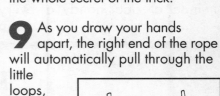

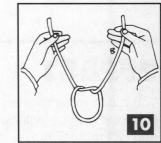

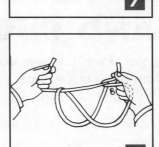

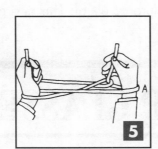

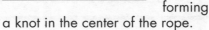

COMMENTS AND SUGGESTIONS

All through the routine, you should emphasize that you never release the ends of the rope. Yet a knot still appears in the rope. That makes this an IMPOSSIBLE KNOT. Practice the moves until they become smooth and natural. When you present the effect, do each move very slowly, step by step, so the spectators can follow them easily. Your purpose is to show the spectators exactly how to do it—except for the final toss where you secretly release the right end of the rope, enabling you to produce a knot where everyone else fails. Although they copy your moves with ropes of their own, they will always miss at the vital point, making the trick more baffling each time it is repeated.

DO-IT-YOURSELF KNOT

To show the baffled spectators how "easy" the IMPOSSIBLE KNOT really is, you form the preliminary loops with your own rope. You then hand the ends to the spectator before the spectator tosses the rope. When the spectator takes the rope from your hands, the spectator still finds that a knot has mysteriously appeared!

METHOD

1 Simply go through all of the preliminary Steps 1 through 5 of the IMPOSSIBLE KNOT, to the point where you have the two ends projecting from each hand with the loops still around your wrists.

2 Extend your hands and invite the spectator to take the ends of the rope, one end in each hand, and draw them apart. When the spectator does, the knot will make its puzzling appearance!

COMMENTS AND SUGGESTIONS

The neat feature here is that the secret move is not necessary. The mere transfer of the ends to the spectator, before you toss the rope off, sets up the formation of the knot. You can further emphasize that the ends of the rope are never released, just as with the IMPOSSIBLE KNOT.

Having shown the spectator how easy it is, you can revert back to the original IMPOSSIBLE KNOT routine. The spectator will again find it impossible to form a knot.

Here, you can offer further help by having the spectator go through the preliminary moves with a rope. You then say to the spectator, "I think you've got it!" Now you take the ends and take the rope from the spectator's hands to show the knot. Give the spectator back the rope, and tell the spectator to start again now that it is obvious that the spectator can do it. But when the spectator tries, there is failure as usual! This is a great party trick. Just have a number of ropes handy, as everyone will want to try it!

TURNED-UP GLASSES

EFFECT

You place three glasses in a row on the table and announce that you will turn over two glasses at a time, and that in three moves you will have them all facing mouth up. Without hesitation you proceed to do just as you said. At the end of the third move, all three glasses are mouth up. This seems easy enough to accomplish; yet every time the spectators try to duplicate your actions, something goes wrong. They always finish with the three glasses mouth down! No matter how often you repeat the effect, the spectators are unable to arrive at the same result as you and are left totally puzzled as to the reason why.

METHOD

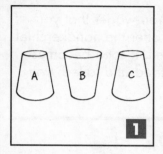

1 Arrange the three glasses in the position shown here. Cups A and C are mouth down at both ends of the row, and cup B is mouth up between them. With the cups in this position, the stunt is really quite easy to accomplish. What the spectators do not realize is that when you let them try it, the three glasses are not in this same starting position, although it seems that they are.

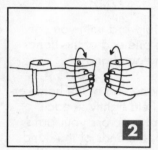

2 To perform the feat, turn your hands thumbs down and grasp the two glasses at your right (B and C) and turn them over, as shown.

3 The arrangement of the glasses should now appear as shown in the illustration. This completes move number one.

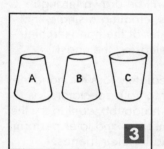

4 Again, start thumbs down and grasp the two glasses at both ends of the row (cups A and C) and turn them over as well.

5 The cups should be positioned as shown here. This completes move number two.

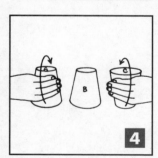

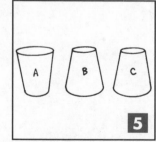

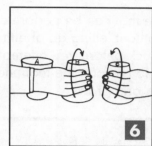

6 Finally, grasp the two glasses at the right (B and C) and turn them over, just as you did in move number one.

7 This completes move number three. All three glasses are now mouth up. You have performed the stunt, as you said you would, in only three moves.

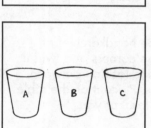

8 Now for the dirty work. To position the cups for the spectator to try, simply turn over the center glass, as shown. Remember, when you performed the stunt you started with one up and two down—and that will work. But one down and two up will not! Therefore, with the cups arranged as shown here, the spectator never will be able to perform the feat with the same results as you.

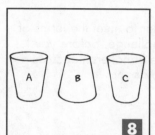

9 If the spectator follows the series of moves exactly as you did, the spectator will be left with the three glasses facing bottoms up, as shown here.

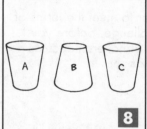

10 By turning over the center glass when all three are in this position, you regain your original position, and your moves are ready-made.

11 Then turn down the center glass, leaving the end ones up, and the spectator is doomed to failure once again.

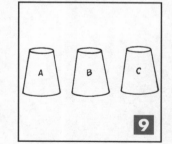

COMMENTS AND SUGGESTIONS

If you perform the stunt too many times, it is possible that your spectators will begin to catch on to the fact that you are changing the arrangement of the cups. It is usually best to do it just once; then let others try and fail. Give another quick demonstration later, but let others worry in the meantime. Use discretion in determining how many times to perform it for the same spectators. You can vary your moves, starting with the two at the left instead of the right, if you wish, but speed is the factor that counts. People are then less likely to note the difference at the start, thanks to your casual turnover of the middle glass.

KNOT IN HANDKERCHIEF

EFFECT

Here is a quick and easy challenge that can be performed anywhere with any handkerchief. You wager that you can tie a knot in a handkerchief without letting go of either end in the process. With that, you offer the handkerchief to anyone who wishes to try their luck before you attempt the seemingly impossible task yourself. It soon becomes quite apparent that no one is able to perform the feat under those conditions. When all have tried and failed, you cleverly perform the stunt with ease and grace.

METHOD

1 Hold the handkerchief at opposite corners and twirl it in a rope-like fashion between your hands. Place it on the table directly in front of you.

2 In order to meet the terms of the challenge, before you pick up the handkerchief cross your arms, as shown.

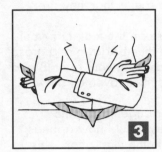

3 Lean forward until you can grasp one end of the hand-kerchief in each hand.

4 With one end of the handker-chief held tightly in each hand, simply uncross your arms. As you do, the ends of the handkerchief will be drawn through your arms, creating a single knot in the center of the handkerchief—without releasing the ends!

5 Immediately toss the handker-chief to your spectators, as they will, no doubt, want to try the stunt themselves and later perform this Betcha for their friends.

CHAPTER 3

CARD MAGIC

Nothing is more perfectly suited for Instant Magic than an ordinary deck of playing cards. Cards are used in children's games such as Go Fish, in casinos around the world for high-stakes gambling, and in neighborhood poker games. Chances are you have a deck on hand at home. If not, you can buy playing cards in almost any supermarket, drugstore, or convenience store.

Because cards are so versatile, they can be used for complex and simple tricks alike. Just think . . . in one deck there are 52 different cards. There are four suits in two colors, and each suit has 13 cards of differing values. Card backs come in different patterns, pictures, and colors. For magical purposes, cards can be crumpled, folded, and torn into pieces.

Hundreds of card tricks have been created around each of these different attributes of cards. From the moment you start performing card tricks, you naturally acquire a manipulative ability that allows you to stay a step ahead of keen-eyed spectators. With technique and practice, you can successfully master the Instant Magic card tricks in this section and amaze audiences everywhere.

AUTOMATIC CARD DISCOVERY

EFFECT

Perhaps one of the most puzzling of all card effects is when a magician causes a selected card to reverse itself and appear face up among the face-down cards in the deck. Here is one of the most basic and yet most effective means of accomplishing this feat.

SECRET AND PREPARATION

Simplicity is the answer here. The trick depends upon having the bottom card of the deck reversed from the start.

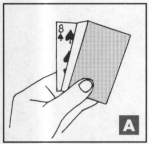

A This can be set up before-hand with the deck in its box, or it can be executed easily and quickly at the moment when the spectators' eyes leave your hands.

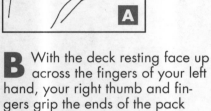

B With the deck resting face up across the fingers of your left hand, your right thumb and fingers grip the ends of the pack from below, as shown. Slide the

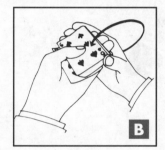

pack toward the tips of your left fingers, at the same time tilting or rotating the deck up on its left edge. This leaves the lone card—in this case the eight of spades—still resting on your left fingers.

C Continue the rotary motion until the right hand has turned the pack face down on the eight of spades, which thus, without the spectators knowing it, has become a face-up card at the bottom of the pack. You are now ready to present the trick.

METHOD

1 Spread the cards in your hands face down so that a spectator has an opportunity to freely select any card from the deck. Care must be taken here not to spread the cards too near the bottom of the deck, to avoid accidentally flashing the face-up bottom card.

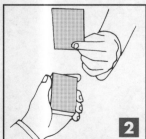

2 As soon as the card is selected by the spectator, square up the deck in your left hand and ask the spectator to look at the card.

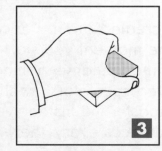

3 At the moment when the spectator's eyes are focusing on the card, the left hand turns com-

pletely over and sets the deck of cards on the table. This action turns all of the cards in the deck face up, except for the "bottom" card which is now face down. Because of this single reversed card, it appears that the deck is still face down.

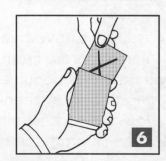

4 Leave the deck sitting on the table, as you tell the spectator to show the card to the other spectators.

5 When the spectator has shown the card, pick up the deck, in its secretly reversed position, with your left hand. Particular care must be taken here to keep the deck squared up so as not to flash the face-up pack below the top, single reversed card.

6 Holding the deck firmly, ask the spectator to push the card face down anywhere in the deck. Unknown to the spectator, the card is really being put into a face-up deck. (Except for the top card.)

7 When the spectator has inserted the card into the deck, place the deck behind your back and explain that since the spectator touched only one card in the deck, that card will be a bit warmer than the other cards. State that, due to your highly trained sense of touch, you will be able to find the card and reveal it in a startling way.

8 When you place the deck behind your back, simply turn over the single reversed card and replace it face up on the deck. Now, every card in the deck is facing in the same direction, *except* the spectator's card. It is the only reversed card in the deck.

SUPER AUTOMATIC CARD DISCOVERY

 In performing the AUTOMATIC CARD DISCOVERY, here is another very easy and clever method for reversing the bottom card and secretly turning over the pack.

METHOD

1 It is not necessary to have the bottom card reversed before the start of the trick.

2 After the spectator has selected a card from the deck, tell the spectator to remember the card. Announce that after the card is replaced in the deck, you are going to place the deck behind your back and locate the card in a very startling fashion.

3 Place the deck behind your back. Turn the bottom card face up. Turn the whole pack over so that it is all face up, except for the one face-down card on top.

4 Bring the deck out from behind your back. You are now ready for the spectator to replace the card in the pack.

COMMENTS AND SUGGESTIONS

With this method, you can perform the trick at any time with no preparation. The spectator may even shuffle the deck before freely selecting a card. It only takes a moment to set up the pack behind your back as you "demonstrate" the first part of the startling way in which you are going to find the spectator's card. However, when you do this "demonstration," do not tell the spectator that the card will later be discovered face up in a face-down pack, or you may alert the spectators to your secret. This method not only allows you to reverse the bottom card, but also to turn the pack over for the replacement of the selected card without any tricky moves whatsoever. When you first place the deck behind your back, just do it naturally, as if you were illustrating what is going to happen next. You can now present a very puzzling, self-working card trick that appears to require great skill yet is practically automatic in every respect.

FANTASTIC FIVE

EFFECT

This is a clever, self-working card discovery utilizing a prepared deck in its simplest form. The trick finishes with a double twist that will leave the onlookers completely baffled. Adding one surprise onto another is always a good policy, especially with card tricks.

A card is freely selected by a spectator and returned to the top of the deck. The pack is then given a cut. You spread the pack on the table, revealing that one card is face up. It is a five. You explain that the face-up card, the five, is your magical indicator card. Then you count down five cards in the deck below where the face-up card was located. Turning up the fifth card, it proves to be the card chosen by the spectator! If that were not enough, you now turn the four cards that were between the face-up card and the spectator's card. All four are aces!

SECRET AND PREPARATION

To prepare, run through the pack and remove the four aces and a five-card. Square up the pack and place the five face up on the bottom of the face-down pack. Place the four aces face down below the five.

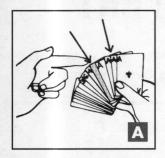

A The first illustration shows the proper preparation with the pack held face up.

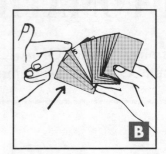

B This shows the pack held in its normal face-down position. Square up the pack and you're ready to begin.

METHOD

1 Spread the pack and invite a spectator to select a card. Be sure not to spread the pack too near the bottom, thereby accidentally exposing the face-up five.

2 Tell the spectator to be sure to remember the card. Square up the deck and place it on the table.

3 Ask the spectator to place the card on top of the deck.

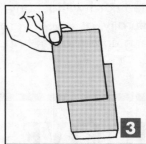

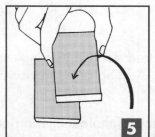

4 Have the spectator cut the deck.

5 Let the spectator complete the cut.

NOTE: Unknown to the spectator, when the deck is cut, the four aces and the face-up five are placed directly above the selected card.

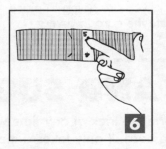

6 Explain to the spectator that something magical is going to happen. At the same time, spread the deck, face down, on the table. Call attention to the one face-up card in the deck.

7 Separate all the cards to the right of the face-up five.

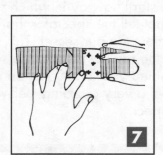

8 Explain that the face-up card is your magical indicator card and that it will help to locate the card the spectator selected. Since the card is a five, that must be a clue. Count down five cards in the deck.

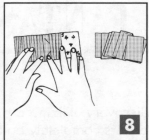

9 Push the five, the four face-down aces below it, and the next card (the spectator's card) all forward from the pack.

10 Turn over the fifth card and show it to be the card that the spectator selected.

11 The spectator will assume that the trick is over. Not content with this, you turn over the four remaining cards to reveal the four aces. This second, added surprise, the appearance of the aces, adds greatly to the effect. This is also a good lead-in to any four-ace trick.

COMMENTS AND SUGGESTIONS

Here is another presentation idea. After the spectator has returned the selected card to the pack and completed the cut, pick up the deck and give it a snap before you spread it along the table. Say that this will cause a card to turn over somewhere in the deck. When the spread reveals the face-up five, count down to the chosen card. Turn it over, revealing it to be the spectator's selected card. Now for the added touch. Gather up the upper and lower portions of the pack, placing the "aces" half of the deck on top. Say, "Wherever I snap the pack a second time, something good always turns up,". . . SNAP! . . . "like the four aces!" Then, deal the four aces from the top of the deck, turning each ace face up as you place it on the table.

TURNOVER CARD

This surprising effect is performed with a pack of ordinary playing cards. It can be done with a borrowed deck and requires no skill or practice. The trick depends on the use of a key card, which is one of the most basic and simple methods used in card magic to locate a selected card in a pack of cards.

EFFECT

You have a spectator shuffle a pack of cards and cut the cards anywhere the spectator wishes. Tell the spectator to look at the card that was cut to and then complete the cut, thus burying the card in the deck. At this point, you take the cards in your hands for the first time and proceed to find the selected card.

SECRET AND PREPARATION

The secret of the trick depends entirely upon the performer secretly learning the bottom card of the pack before it is placed on the table to begin the trick. This card is called a key card because it will be your key to the location of the selected card. In the following description, we will assume that your key card (the card on the bottom of the deck) is the two of clubs.

METHOD

1 If you use a pack of cards that is already in its case at the start, you can glimpse the bottom card as you remove the cards from the case. Just lay the pack face down and go right into the trick without a shuffle.

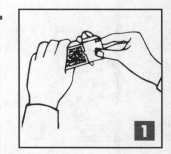

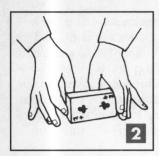

2 Even better, if people want to shuffle the pack, let them. Often when a spectator is squaring up the pack after shuffling, he will flash the bottom card in your direction, not realizing it has anything to do with the trick.

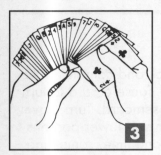

3 If you don't get a glimpse of the card during the shuffle, pick up the pack in your hands, turn it face up, and begin running the cards from hand to hand, as shown.

Comment that the deck appears to be well-shuffled, and it would be impossible for you to know their order. Of course, here you see and remember your key card. Lay the pack face down on the table and you're ready to begin.

4 With the pack lying face down on the table and the audience satisfied that the cards are well-mixed, ask a spectator to divide the pack into two parts.

5 Tell the spectator to cut anywhere in the deck and to place the upper portion on the table.

NOTE: The card that the spectator has cut to, which will be the selected card, is marked with an "X" in the illustrations to make it easier for you to follow. Of course, when you perform the trick, there will be no "X" on the card.

Spectator Looks At Card

6 After the cards have been cut, tell the spectator to remove the top card of the lower half, look at it, remember it, and place it on top of the other half of the pack. Let's assume that the card is the five of diamonds.

7 Point to the lower half and ask the spectator to put those cards on top of the selected card so that it will be buried somewhere in the pack.

NOTE: In placing the lower half on top of the upper half, the spectator is also placing your key card

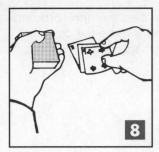

directly above the chosen card. Ask the spectator to give the pack another complete cut.

8 When this is done, take the pack and begin dealing cards one by one on the table, turning each card face up. Announce that you are trying to get an impression of the selected card, but that the spectator is not to say anything, even if the selected card appears, or you will have to begin all over.

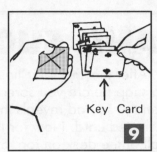

Key Card

9 As you deal cards one at a time from the pack, turning each face up, watch for your key card, the two of clubs. When it shows up, deal it on the table along with the others. You now know that the next card will be the spectator's card (the five of diamonds).

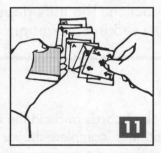

Selected Card

10 Deal the next card, the five of diamonds, but instead of stopping, just continue dealing as if you haven't reached the chosen card.

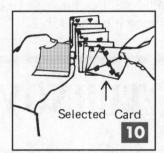

11 After you have dealt several more cards, tell the spectator you have received an impression. Say, "The next card I turn over will be your card." The spectator will probably say you are wrong.

12 But instead of dealing the next card off the pack, reach among the face-up cards on the table and draw out the five of diamonds.

13 Turn over the five and lay it face down on the table, saying, "I said the next card I turned over would be yours—and it is!"

NOTE: This trick is very effective because of its surprise ending! When you deal past the selected card, the spectator is sure that the trick has gone wrong. But when you actually do turn the selected card face down, you really prove your magical powers.

DOUBLE X MYSTERY

EFFECT

Two spectators are invited to assist you. You give the spectator on your left a pack of cards and a pen and ask that spectator to place the pack behind their back and mark an X across the FACE of any card with the pen. You give the same deck and pen to the spectator on your right and ask that spectator to mark the BACK of any card, with the pack behind the spectator. You return the deck to the spectator on your left and ask that spectator to run through the deck and find the card with the X on the FACE, remove it, and hold it between both hands so that it is out of sight. This done, the spectator on the right is again given the deck and asked to find their card, the one with the X on the BACK. Upon searching through the deck, the spectator on the right finds that the card is missing. When the spectator on the left turns the card over, it is found to have an X on the BACK. It appears as if both spectators have chosen and marked the same card!

SECRET AND PREPARATION

The secret to this "coincidence" is so simple it's surprising. It all depends upon the fact that the pen that you give to the spectators just doesn't work. For best results, use a pen with a felt tip. All that is required is to let it sit without the cap on until the tip is dried out. If a pencil is used, it is necessary to dip the top of the pencil in clear varnish and allow it to dry overnight. This will prevent the pencil from making a mark on the cards, although it appears to have a perfectly good point.

To prepare, remove any card from the pack and mark an X on both sides with a pen or pencil that really works and matches the special one you will use in the trick. The lines that form the X should appear irregular, as if the mark were made without looking. Place the card back in the deck, and you're ready.

METHOD

1 With two spectators to assist you, give the deck, face up, to the spectator on your left. Ask this spectator to place the deck behind their back, to run through the cards, and without looking at it, to bring any card to the top of the deck.

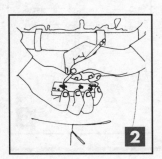

2 When this has been done, give the spectator the prepared pen and instruct the spectator to mark an X across the face of the card and then return the pen to you. Ask the spectator to mix the cards behind their back so the marked card is lost somewhere in the deck. Have the spectator hand you the deck.

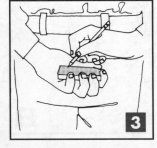

3 Turn the deck face down and hand it to the spectator on your right. Instruct the second spectator just as you did the first spectator. But tell this spectator to mark an X on the back of any card and mix the cards.

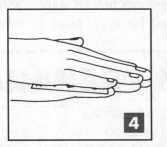

4 Take back the deck and put the pen away. Give the deck again to the spectator on your left, and ask this spectator to look through the cards face up and remove the card the spectator marked from the deck. Have the spectator hold this card between the palms of the hands so no one else can see the card. Actually, the reason for doing this is so that no one sees the X on the back of this card.

NOTE: Because of the prepared pen, neither spectator has made a mark on any card, and both are unaware of the prepared X card in the deck.

5 Give the deck to the spectator on your right and ask this spectator to do the same: "Please run through the deck and remove your card, the one with the X on the back." Of course, the spectator will be unable to find the card.

6 After several attempts, call attention to the fact that the only card missing from the deck is the one that the other spectator is holding. Tell the spectator on your left to look at the back of the card. It appears that the two spectators were somehow able to freely select and mark the very same card in the deck!

COMMENTS AND SUGGESTIONS

It is a good idea at the start of the trick to run through the cards face up and show them to be an ordinary deck. In order to do this, it is necessary to have the secret X card close to the bottom of the deck. Then, run through the cards face up, supposedly to show that they are all different. Just be careful not to spread the cards near the position in the deck where the X card is located. The spectator will believe everything is on the up-and-up. You will be amazed at the effect that this trick has, as there appears to be no reasonable explanation for the astonishing results. Properly performed, no one will ever suspect the special pen is the secret to the mystery.

SUPER DOUBLE X MYSTERY

One very subtle convincer, which can make this trick a complete baffler, is to introduce a duplicate pen (the one that really made the X on the card), after the prepared pen has done the dirty work. Simply have the duplicate in your pocket and, after the second spectator has made a "mark," casually place the pen in the pocket with the duplicate. As the second spectator is looking for the card with the X, remove the unprepared pen and help the spectator search by pointing to various parts of the deck with the real pen. Then just lay the pen somewhere in plain sight. Now everything can be examined.

SUPER ANYTIME DOUBLE X MYSTERY

With this method, you can perform the DOUBLE X MYSTERY at any time during your card routine, even though the deck has been used for a number of other tricks and even examined by the spectators!

SECRET AND PREPARATION

Before you begin, place the X-marked card either (A) under your belt behind your back or (B) in a gimmick card holder made from a safety pin and a paper clip. The special card is placed in the paper clip and the holder pinned inside the back of your coat (C) so that the card is just hidden by the bottom edge of your coat.

 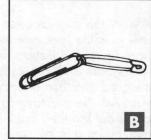 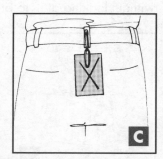

METHOD

1 Have one of the spectators shuffle the deck. Then place the deck behind your back to illustrate to the spectators what they are to do. At this time, you secretly remove the X card from beneath your coat and add it to the deck!

2 You are ready to proceed with the SUPER DOUBLE X MYSTERY, as previously described.

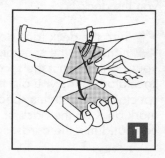 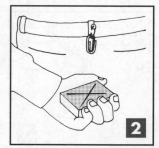

YOU DO AS I DO

As a "two person" trick, this is a real baffler. All you need are two ordinary decks of playing cards. It is a good idea to use packs with different colors on their backs, so that the spectators can keep track of them as the trick proceeds.

EFFECT

Two packs of cards are thoroughly shuffled. One is shuffled by a spectator, and you shuffle the other pack. You and the spectator then exchange packs, and each selects a card, taking care that the other person does not see it. The cards are both replaced in their decks. You and the spectator exchange decks again, and each finds the duplicate of the card selected in the other pack. You and the spectator then place the selected cards face down on the table. When the two cards are turned up, they prove to be identical!

SECRET AND PREPARATION

This is one of the finest self-working tricks in card magic. You need only two ordinary decks of cards. The trick can be performed anytime, anywhere, with no previous preparation. Let's assume that one deck has red backs and the other blue.

METHOD

1 Place both decks on the table and ask the spectator to select either one. This is a free choice. Let's assume that the spectator takes the deck with the red backs. This leaves you with the blue-backed deck.

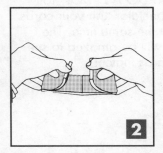

Key Card

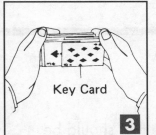

2 Tell the spectator to "do as I do." Shuffle your blue deck, and the spectator should do the same with the red deck.

3 As you complete the last shuffle, square up your deck, as shown in the picture. As you do, turn the deck on its edge, glimpse the bottom card, and remember it. Do not call attention to this, just remember the bottom card, as it will serve as your key card for the rest of the trick.

NOTE: In the illustration, the eight of diamonds will be your key card.

4 Stress to the spectator that, to make sure that all is fair, you will trade decks, so you will be using a deck that the spectator personally has shuffled. Exchange decks with the spectator. Unknown to the spectator, you know the bottom card of the blue deck the spectator now holds.

5 Instruct the spectator to fan open the blue deck, holding the deck up, so that you cannot see the faces, just as you are doing with the red deck. The spectator is to freely select any card from the deck, and you will do likewise. Tell the spectator it's best if the spectator selects a favorite card, and that you will do the same and select your favorite card.

NOTE: To make the illustrations easy to follow, we have marked the spectator's card with an X.

Magician **5**

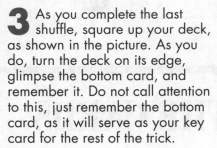
Spectator **5**

6 Ask the spectator to place the selected card on the top of the deck, as shown, as you do the same with your card. It is not necessary for you to remember the card that you have selected at this point. Just remember your key card, the one that is on the bottom of the deck now held by the spectator—the eight of diamonds.

Magician **6**

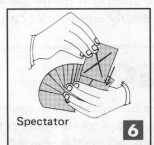
Spectator **6**

 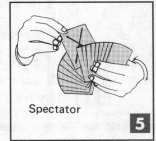

7 Have the spectator square up the cards, as you do the same. Each of you places your deck on the table.

Magician

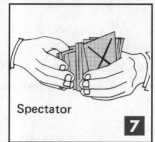

Spectator

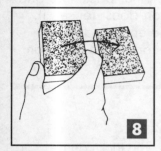

8 Tell the spectator to cut the deck, as you cut your deck, thus burying the selected cards somewhere in the middle of each pack. Unknown to the spectator, this cut places the bottom card, which is your key card (the eight of diamonds), directly above the spectator's selected card.

9 Have the spectator complete the cut and ask the spectator to cut one more time, as you do the same. Be sure that each cut is a single cut and that the cut is completed each time.

10 Stress the fact that there's no possible way that you could know where the spectator's favorite card is now located in the deck, and, likewise, the spectator could not know where your card is.

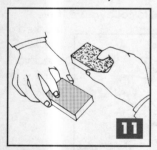

11 Trade decks with the spectator once more. You now hold the one you originally shuffled, the blue deck with your key card.

12 Have the spectator look through the red deck and remove the card which matches

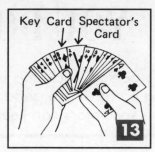

Key Card   Spectator's Card

the spectator's favorite card, and you will do the same with the blue deck.

13 While the spectator does this, you spread your deck until you locate your key card, the eight of diamonds. The card immediately to the right of the key card will be the card the spectator selected.

14 Tell the spectator to remove the selected card without showing its face, and you will do the same. Actually, you remove the card which you now know to be the one the spectator selected, the two of clubs.

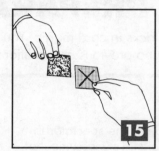

15 Have the spectator place the card on the table, and you place yours beside it.

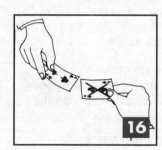

16 Say, "It would be quite a coincidence if we both had the same favorite card, wouldn't it?" Again, stress the fact that you each have been doing the same thing: YOU DO AS I DO. You and the spectator turn your cards face up at the same time. The spectator will be amazed to see that the cards match!

SPRINGING THE CARDS

This fancy flourish is the basis for many other flourishes with a pack of cards. It is one that should be practiced first on a limited scale (SPRINGING THE CARDS only a short distance) with a pack that can be handled easily and comfortably. Then you can gradually increase the scope of this manipulation.

EFFECT

You hold a pack of cards lengthwise between your thumb and fingers. By applying steady pressure on the pack, you cause all the cards in the pack to spring in succession from one hand to the other—in midair! This has a very impressive effect on the spectators, as the cards form a colorful cascade that can cover a surprising distance.

METHOD

1 Hold the pack lengthwise in your right hand, with your thumb at the lower end and your first, second, and third fingers at the upper end. The pack should be held close to the tips of the fingers, as shown.

2 Your left hand is held palm up with the fingers spread wide, pointing upward. This forms a sort of trap to catch the cards as they cascade from the right hand into the left.

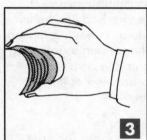

3 With the pack held firmly in your right hand, squeeze your thumb and fingers together, bending the cards inward toward the palm of your hand, and move the right hand about 3" above the cupped left hand.

4 Continue to squeeze the pack inward as you begin to release the cards from the tips of your right fingers, sending them

springing, one by one, from the right hand into the left hand.

NOTE: The left hand should be positioned so that, as the cards arrive in the hand, the outer ends of the cards hit the left first fingers, preventing them from shooting out of the hand onto the floor.

5 As the cards start to spring from one hand to the other, gradually begin drawing your right hand farther away, a few inches at first, then more and more. No matter what distance you will eventually achieve, always begin with your hands close together. Then draw the right hand away, as the cards spring into your left hand.

6 When the bulk of the pack has arrived in your left hand, and only a few cards remain in the right, move your right hand toward your left hand, gathering all the cards in between to conclude the flourish.

COMMENTS AND SUGGESTIONS

In practicing the spring, place your left hand just below your right hand and spring the pack for a distance of only a few inches. Your purpose is to gain the knack of springing the cards smoothly and evenly without losing any of them. Once you learn to release the cards in an even stream, with practice you can then spread your hands a foot or so apart. When you first practice, it is best to use soft, flexible cards; an old, used deck works well.

It is also a good idea to practice over a bed, as a certain amount of failure is inevitable at first. One final suggestion: If you swing your body from left to right during the spring, the distance effect between your hands is further exaggerated, creating the illusion that the cards cover a distance of 18" to 2'.

ARM-SPREAD CATCH

One of the most spectacular of card flourishes, this also appears to be one of the most difficult. Proper technique, attention to detail, and a reasonable amount of practice combine to produce impressive results in this special branch of magic that blends juggling with wizardry.

EFFECT

You spread a pack of cards lengthwise along your left arm from the base of your fingers to your elbow. With the cards neatly set in place, you give your arm an upward toss and at the same time make a long, inward sweep with your right hand, scooping up the entire pack of cards in midair without dropping a single card.

METHOD

1 Hold the pack in your right hand, with your thumb at one end and your fingers at the other. Extend your left arm, palm up, and hold the pack slightly above the fingers of your left hand. Bend the entire pack inward toward the right palm (the same type of bending by the right hand as used in SPRINGING THE CARDS).

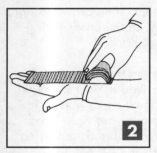

2 Slowly begin to release the cards from the tips of the right fingers onto the left hand. At the same time, move your right hand down the length of your left arm. The cards should begin forming an even spread along your left arm.

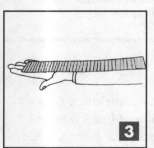

3 Continue releasing the cards from your fingertips along the left arm until all the cards have been spread. With practice, you can attain a spread that extends from the tips of your left fingers to your elbow.

NOTE: After the cards are spread along the arm, it is necessary to keep the arm very still in order to prevent the cards from falling.

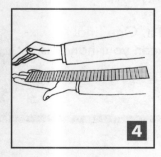

4 With the cards neatly set in place, position your cupped right hand near your left fingertips, at the beginning of the spread, in readiness to catch the cards.

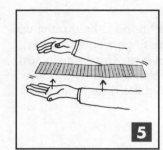

5 With an upward lifting and tossing motion of your left arm, gently throw the entire spread of cards into the air, as shown.

6 Without hesitation, and in one continuous movement, swing your entire body to the left and, with a long sweeping motion of the right hand, begin gathering or scooping up the cards in midair, from one end of the spread to the other.

7 With practice you should be able to catch the entire pack without any cards falling to the floor. At first, practice the ARM-SPREAD CATCH using half of a pack and a shorter arm spread. Gradually add more cards until you can perform the flourish with a full pack that is spread from the tips of the fingers to the elbow.

COMMENTS AND SUGGESTIONS

In early trials, as you practice springing the cards along the arm, the spread may prove too irregular for an effective catch. In that case simply lower your left arm rapidly and let the pack slide down into your cupped left hand. This is a neat manipulation in itself, so you can use it as a preliminary warm-up before the catch.

THE WATERFALL

EFFECT

You grasp the entire pack in your right hand with your left hand cupped beneath it. Skillfully you begin to release the cards in rapid succession, causing them to cascade downward, one at a time, like a waterfall into your waiting left hand. The flourish reaches its conclusion after the entire pack has made its impressive journey through the air into your left hand.

METHOD

1 Grasp and hold the deck lengthwise in your right hand with your thumb at one end of the pack and your four fingers at the other end. Your right fingers and thumb should be straight with only the edges of the top card touching your right hand.

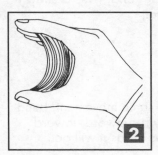

2 Keeping your fingers and thumb straight, slowly squeeze them together so that the cards bend inward toward your right palm. This action is very similar to SPRINGING THE CARDS, except here the object is to get a small amount of space between each and every card, as you hold the pack.

3 The special grip described here allows the ends of the cards to spread along the length of your thumb and fingers. Performed correctly, the cards should fill up all the open space between your thumb and fingers. Careful practice will teach you just how to bend the pack to secure this small gap between the individual cards.

4 With the cards held in this manner, you are ready to begin THE WATERFALL. Position your cupped left hand directly below your right hand, in readiness to receive the cards as they fall. The illustration shows the proper position of both hands at the beginning of the flourish. This and all of the following steps are shown from the spectators' point of view.

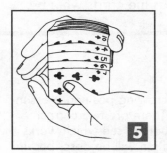

5 Slowly begin to spread open your right thumb and fingers, releasing the cards in succession from the face of the pack. This action causes the cards to fall into the left hand in an even flow.

6 At the same time, move your left hand downward as the cards continue to fall from your right hand. If you release the cards in an even flow, they will resemble a waterfall as they cascade from one hand to the other.

7 To achieve maximum distance between your hands, move your right hand up a few inches at the same time you move your left hand down. With practice you can attain a "waterfall" of 8" to 12", or even longer.

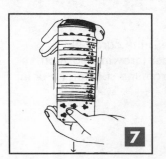

8 When nearly all the cards have been released from your right hand, quickly move your hands back together, squaring up the cards, to complete the flourish. You are now prepared to repeat THE WATERFALL as many times as you wish. The spectators will be more than convinced that you possess great skill as a card manipulator.

COMMENTS AND SUGGESTIONS

The real secret of THE WATERFALL is your initial grip on the pack, as shown in Steps 1 and 2. The cards must be spread evenly along your thumb and fingers. At the start, practice the flourish with your hands very close together. Then as you begin to acquire the knack necessary to release the cards in an even stream, move your hands farther apart. When selecting cards to use for this flourish, it is a good idea to experiment with different decks. Choose cards that bend easily enough for you to space them evenly in your hand. If you practice this flourish with a deck that suits you well, you will be pleased at the progress you will make in achieving a perfect waterfall effect.

THROWING A CARD

Many famous magicians have intrigued spectators throughout the world with their ability to sail cards to the highest balconies of the largest theaters. How far you can go toward achieving a similar result will depend on how much practice you are willing to devote to this very impressive flourish.

EFFECT

Upon concluding your card routine, you offer several cards for examination by sailing them across the room to different spectators. This is done in a smooth, graceful manner, sending the cards skimming into the air while the spectators watch in amazement as the cards whiz by.

METHOD

1 Holding the card in the proper throwing position is essential in attaining effective results. There are two correct positions, and you should try them both to see which works best for you. (The other holding position will be described in the next effect, the BOOMERANG CARD.)

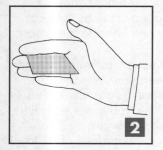

2 To place the card in the first position, clip the very end of the card between the first and second fingers of your right hand, as shown. Do not allow the card to droop. Hold it firmly so that it is level with the fingers at all times.

3 Here is the card held in proper throwing position, as seen from the spectators' point of view.

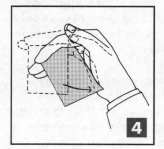

4 Start by bending all four fingers inward, until the lower right edge of the card touches the heel of your hand. (This is shown from above.)

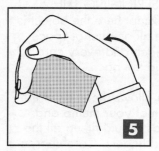

5 In the same movement, bend your wrist inward, toward yourself, as far as it will go.

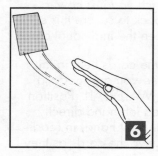

6 To make the actual throw, snap your wrist open, as hard as you can. At the same time, straighten out your fingers and release the card to send it spinning out of your hand.

COMMENTS AND SUGGESTIONS

Keeping the card level with your fingers and maintaining a consistent wrist action are essential factors in developing the throw, which can cover a long range once the knack is acquired. When aiming for higher levels, the hand must be kept on target, and the force of throw increased. Along with accuracy, the practiced performer can propel the cards an impressive distance by combining a throwing motion of the arm with the action of the wrist, as a means of gaining still greater distance.

BOOMERANG CARD

After demonstrating your skill by throwing playing cards great distances to the spectators, you begin throwing cards toward the ceiling—only to have them sail out into the air and return to your hand, much like a boomerang.

METHOD

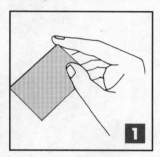

1 In order to achieve the boomerang effect, the card should be held either in the position described in THROWING A CARD or in this new position as follows: Hold the card at one end between the tips of the right thumb and fingers, as shown. Grip the card near the outer right corner between your right thumb and second finger. Your first finger rests against the left corner of the card, to serve as a pivot point to start the spinning action of the card as it leaves the hand.

2 With the card held in this position, it can be sent spinning out of the hand using the same arm and wrist action as described in THROWING A CARD.

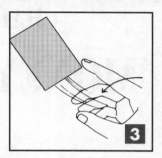

3 To achieve the boomerang effect, hold the card in either throwing position. Instead of throwing the card out of the hand on a level plane, throw it at an upward angle of 45° or more, with just enough force to send it only a few yards away from you. In throwing the card, concentrate on obtaining as much spin as possible. This is done by snapping your hand back toward your body just before you release the card. Your first finger on the outer right corner acts as the pivot point, to aid in starting the card in its spin as it leaves your right hand.

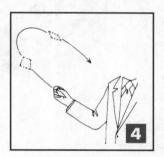

4 Once the card has reached its maximum distance in the air and begins its downward fall, it will return to you instead of falling straight down to the floor. This is due to the 45-degree angle of the card in the air. With practice, you will be able to cause the card to return directly to your hand, where you can catch it between your thumb and fingers.

COMMENTS AND SUGGESTIONS

Practice the BOOMERANG CARD until it can be done with neatness and precision. Performed properly, it creates an impression of great skill and dexterity. A certain amount of failure is inevitable at first, but once you develop the knack of THROWING A CARD, this effect should come quickly and easily.

CHAPTER 4

MONEY MAGIC

Tricks with coins and dollar bills are not only baffling but also quite impressive. When you show both hands empty, and then reach out into the air and pluck a number of tens or twenties from nowhere, respect for your magical powers will increase greatly.

Money magic can be performed almost anywhere and under almost any conditions—if you do the right thing. Magically producing money from the air is just as effective in Moscow or Singapore as it is at your local McDonald's. You don't even need to speak the audience's language for them to be impressed. As the old saying goes, money talks.

Whether performing feats of surprising wizardry or impromptu work, stress the fact that you are using ordinary items. Whenever possible, borrow money from spectators, thus proving that skill, not trickery, is the great factor in your work. The more you have your audience believing that, the more fascinating your money magic will appear.

COIN FOLD

EFFECT

You borrow a coin from a spectator, who marks it for later identification. A small sheet of paper is then folded around the coin so it is completely enclosed within the paper. This little package can even be tapped on the table so the spectators can hear that the coin is actually inside. At all times, the folded paper remains in view of the spectators; but you cause the coin to vanish from within the paper, which you tear into pieces. You then produce the coin from your pocket, the spectator's lapel, or anywhere you wish.

SECRET AND PREPARATION

No special items are required for this effect. The coin, however, should be large enough for an effective vanish. A half-dollar or dollar-sized coin works well and is easily visible even at some distance. The piece of paper used should measure approximately 4" x 6".

METHOD

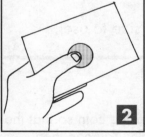

1 Borrow a coin from a spectator and have the spectator mark the coin with a permanent-ink marking pen for later identification. Hold the paper in your left hand and display the coin openly in your right fingertips. You remark, "I will seal the borrowed coin with the folds of this piece of paper."

2 Place the coin in the center of the paper and hold it there with your left thumb and fingers, as shown.

3 With the right fingers, fold the upper half of the paper toward you, as shown—completely over the coin—so that no part of the coin is visible to you or to the spectators.

4 Fold the left side of the paper away from you, against the back of the coin. This seals the coin in the paper at the left side. Do not fold the paper tightly against the edge of the coin. Instead, leave about ¼" of "play" between the fold and the left edge of the coin.

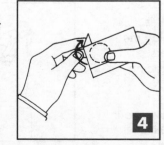

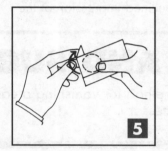

5 Fold the right side of the paper away from you, against the back of the coin so it overlaps the left-hand fold. This seals the coin in the paper from the right side. Again, leave ¼" of "play" between the crease of the right fold and the right edge of the coin.

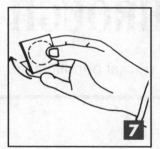

6 At this point, the coin is sealed in on all sides except for the bottom edge of the paper, which remains open. In making the folds, be sure to maintain enough pressure on the coin through the paper to keep it inside, so that it doesn't slide out the open bottom edge.

7 The last fold is the most important. If you folded the bottom edge upward—toward you—it would seal the coin inside. Instead, the last fold is made upward—but toward the spectators. This leaves the bottom edge of the package open, providing a means of escape for the coin.

8 When the last fold has been made, press the paper firmly around the edge of the coin, leaving a distinct impression of the coin outlined on the surface of the paper. This impression is important. It will later convince the spectators that the coin is still wrapped securely within the folded package.

9 Hold the small package with the tips of your right fingers. Tap the edge of the folded paper on the table, allowing the spectators to "hear" the coin inside. Say, "The coin is now securely sealed within the folded paper. If you listen, you can even hear it."

10 To make the coin vanish, you hold the folded paper with the "opening" pointing downward, toward the base of your fingers. Relax the pressure of your right thumb and fingers, and the coin will slide out of the bottom of the paper into your right hand, where it remains hidden in your curled fingers.

11 After the coin drops into your hand, take the package with your left fingers. Your right hand falls casually to your side with the coin secretly held in the finger-palm position (see page 47), as shown.

12 With your left hand, casually display the folded package to the spectators, who believe that the coin is still wrapped inside. This is where the outlined impression of the coin becomes so valuable. As you display the paper, casually show both sides, allowing the spectators to see the impression made by the coin, thus proving the presence of the coin.

13 Another way to get rid of the coin is to place your hand casually in your right pants or coat pocket as the folded package is transferred from the right to the left hand, instead of leaving the coin in your right hand. This way, your right hand will be empty as you move on to the next step.

14 Bring both hands together in front of you and tear the paper in half. (The illustration shows how to hold the coin in the finger-palm position as you tear the paper.)

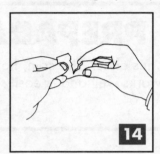

Toss the pieces onto the table. You can even tear the paper into many pieces to prove, without a doubt, that the coin has truly vanished. The coin can then be reproduced from your pocket; or, if you still hold the coin in your hand, you can produce it from the spectator's coat lapel, tie, or anywhere you desire.

COMMENTS AND SUGGESTIONS

The COIN FOLD is a standard method for vanishing a coin and can be used in conjunction with many coin routines where the vanish of a coin is necessary.

COIN THROUGH HANDKERCHIEF I

Here is a clever effect using a pocket handkerchief and a coin (a half-dollar is a good size to use).

EFFECT

You display the coin at the tips of your right thumb and fingers. You drape the handkerchief over the coin so that the coin seems to penetrate the fabric of the handkerchief, without leaving a trace of a tear or a hole. You can then hand a spectator both the coin and the handkerchief for examination.

METHOD

1 For this effect you may use your own handkerchief, but the trick is stronger if you utilize a borrowed one. In either case, first display the coin by holding it at the tips of your right thumb and first two fingers. Your fingers and thumb are pointing up, with one side of the coin facing the spectators.

2 With your left hand, drape the handkerchief over the coin and over your right hand. The coin should be under the center of the handkerchief.

3 With your left hand, adjust the handkerchief around the coin. At the same time, underneath the handkerchief, secretly lift a small bit of cloth behind the coin with your right thumb and fold it around your left thumb, as shown.

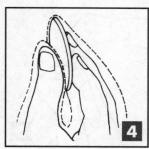

4 Remove your left hand, leaving the small bit of handkerchief nipped between your right thumb and the back of the coin. This places two layers of fabric between the right thumb and the coin.

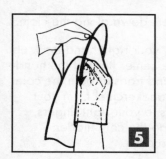

5 Grasp the front edge of the handkerchief with your left hand, lifting it up, back, and completely over the coin. This action will expose the coin to the spectators, supposedly to assure them that the coin is still in its original position.

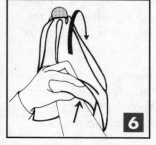

6 The following move is the real secret of the trick. With your left hand, grasp both edges of the handkerchief and lift them both up and over the coin, as shown.

7 The effect on the spectators will be that you simply exposed the coin for them to show that it was still there and then re-covered it with the handkerchief as before.

8 In actuality, you are now holding the coin outside the back of the handkerchief.

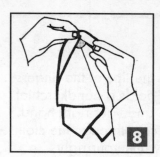

It will appear to the spectators as if the handkerchief is draped completely around the coin.

9 With your left hand, grasp the coin through the now doubled-over fabric and remove your right hand, as shown.

10 With your right hand, twist the lower part of the handkerchief around the coin.

11 As you twist the handkerchief, the shape of the coin will become visible under the fabric.

12 You may also adjust the cloth over the exposed "back" of the coin and show the handkerchief on all sides, if you wish.

13 Slowly push the coin upward in the handkerchief, as your left hand comes over to take the edge of the coin, as it "penetrates" the handkerchief.

14 You may hand both the handkerchief and the coin to a spectator for examination.

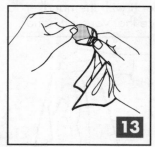

COIN THROUGH HANDKERCHIEF II

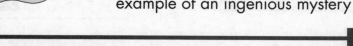

This effect will appear exactly the same to the spectators as the first COIN THROUGH HANDKERCHIEF, yet the method is entirely different. But because it is so direct and bold, it will fool anyone who might know the first method described. This is another example of an ingenious mystery devised by "Gen" Grant.

EFFECT

You display a half-dollar between the tips of the fingers of your right hand. Your left hand holds a handkerchief that you drape over both the coin and your right hand. With your left hand, you grip the coin through the cloth from the outside, holding it there while your right hand is withdrawn from beneath. Your right hand again grasps the coin—this time through the material. Now you move your left hand down and grasp the hanging corners of the handkerchief, while your right hand continues to hold the coin. You give a sharp downward jerk to the handkerchief, and the coin "penetrates" completely through the cloth, leaving no trace of a hole.

METHOD

All of the following illustrations are as seen from your point of view.

1 Hold the coin by the tips of your right finger and thumb, as shown. Pick up the handkerchief with your left hand.

2 As you display the coin, begin to cover it with the handkerchief. Notice that your left hand holds the edge of the handkerchief by the side, not by the corner.

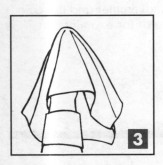

3 When the coin is completely covered, the front edge of the cloth (the edge toward the spectators) drapes a little lower than the back edge. This leaves the handkerchief a bit shorter in back than in front.

4 Your left hand grips the coin through the cloth, from the outside, between the thumb and fingers, as shown.

5 As you withdraw your right hand from beneath the handkerchief, you really keep the coin in your right hand and secretly bring it down below the rear edge of the handkerchief. Your left hand holds the handkerchief at the center, as if it were still holding the coin through the cloth.

6 With your right hand, bring the coin up behind the handkerchief and slide it under your left thumb, clipping the coin behind the cloth, out of the spectators' view.

7 With your right fingers, pretend to adjust the folds of the right side of the handkerchief by sliding

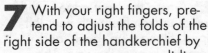

your fingers down along the cloth.

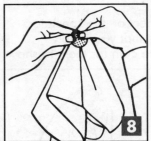

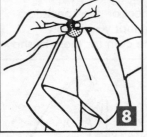

8 Bring your right hand back up to the center (top) of the handkerchief and transfer both the coin and the handkerchief from your left fingers to your right fingers, still keeping the coin hidden behind the cloth.

9 With your left fingers, pretend to adjust the left side of the handkerchief, sliding the fingers down the cloth as before.

10 Gather all four corners of the handkerchief into your left hand. Your right hand still holds the coin behind the cloth.

11 Hold the corners tightly in your left hand. Jerk the handkerchief sharply downward, out of your right hand. Pull the handkerchief away from the coin, which remains held by your right fingertips. The coin has apparently penetrated the center of the handkerchief! The handkerchief and the coin can then be tossed to the spectators for examination.

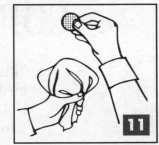

COMMENTS AND SUGGESTIONS

As bold as this may seem, when it is performed correctly every movement is natural and will be accepted by even the sharpest observers, who are looking for quick or suspicious movements. Rehearse it first by actually leaving the coin under the handkerchief and going through the rest of the steps. Then repeat the same actions, following the magical penetration routine given here. When both look the same, you will be ready to present this second version of the COIN THROUGH HANDKERCHIEF.

MAGICALLY MULTIPLY YOUR MONEY

For a neat, close-up effect, this is ideal. It can be set up in a moment and performed almost anywhere, provided the spectators are close enough to fully appreciate it. It makes an excellent close-up trick, but it also can be worked while you are standing.

EFFECT

You display a nickel between the tips of your right thumb and first finger. The other fingers of your right hand are open wide. Everyone can see your hand is empty, except for the nickel.

After showing that your left hand is just as empty, you slowly grasp the nickel with your left thumb and first finger. For a brief moment, both hands hold the coin at the fingertips, then the hands draw apart in a slow, outward motion. The spectators are amazed to see two half-dollars emerging instead of the nickel. When both hands are separated, each unmistakably holds a real half-dollar, proving that your money has multiplied twenty times over. That's magic!

SECRET AND PREPARATION

The entire effect depends upon an artful form of concealment, which is simplicity itself yet so deceptive that no one will suspect it. Skill is reduced to a minimum.

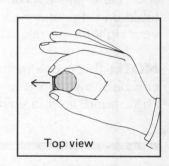

Top view

To prepare, hold the two half-dollars edgewise (horizontally) near the tips of your right thumb and forefinger, keeping the two coins together. Place the nickel upright (vertically) between the tips of the same thumb and forefinger, as illustrated. Center the nickel against the outer edge of the half-dollars. With the coins held firmly in this position, you are ready to begin.

METHOD

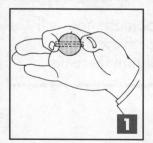

1 As you face the spectators, position your right hand straight at them, showing the nickel at their eye level. The spectators will not see the halves hiding edgewise behind the nickel if, and only if, your hand is held so that the halves are parallel to their line of vision—hidden behind the much smaller nickel. Illustration A shows the starting position as it would be seen from slightly above. Notice how the nickel masks the half-dollars since the edges of the halves are at the exact center of the nickel.

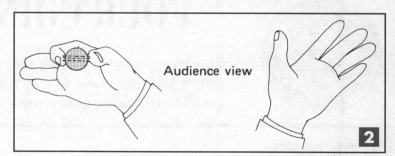

Audience view

2 From the spectators' view, your right hand is so obviously empty (except for the nickel) that any suspicion would be directed toward your left hand, which you show as empty—front and back.

3 Slowly and deliberately, bring your hands together, with the thumbs and forefingers of both hands pointing toward each other. The remaining fingers of both hands should be slightly opened to give the spectator a clear view of your "empty" hands.

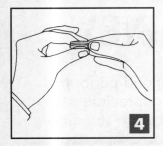

NOTE: Keep your hand level with the spectators' eyes so that they do not see the concealed halves as you turn your hand.

4 As your hands move closer together, your left thumb comes beneath the coins, pushing the lower edge of the nickel inward, rotating the nickel up against the bottom half-dollar. All three coins are now horizontal. This is the one moment when the coins are out of the direct view of the spectators.

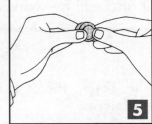

5 All in the same action, tip the three coins upright toward the spectators with your left thumb and first finger. The coins are all held together in a stack, with the nickel hidden in back.

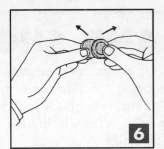

6 Without stopping, grip the stack between your thumbs and fingers and begin drawing the two halves apart. Your left hand draws the front half-dollar to the left, while your right hand draws the rear half-dollar and the nickel to the right.

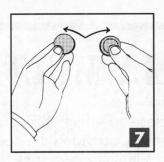

7 Your right thumb keeps the nickel hidden behind the rear half-dollar, retaining it there as you separate the two halves.

To the spectators, the nickel will appear to have magically enlarged and doubled before their eyes—in an instant!

8 The coins are then drawn completely apart and shown as two half-dollars at the fingertips of each hand. Be careful not to accidentally flash the hidden nickel when displaying the two halves to the spectators.

COMMENTS AND SUGGESTIONS

This is a brief but baffling effect. The only question left concerns the disposal of the nickel, which, if seen, would spoil the mystery. When seated at a table, after displaying the half-dollars bring both hands near the edge of the table and dip your right hand a little behind your left hand. This hides your right hand momentarily. At that moment, your right thumb releases the nickel, letting it fall into your lap.

NOTE: This is one method of "lapping." Both hands then come forward and toss their coins on the table. The hands can be shown to be completely empty, proving that the nickel is no longer there. If you are standing, just place the "right-hand" half in your pocket (along with the secret nickel) and proceed with any effect using the "left-hand" half.

FOUR COIN ASSEMBLY

This highly effective table trick is performed with the simplest of objects. You will only need four coins (either half-dollars or quarters), two pieces of 3" x 5" cardboard (index cards work nicely), and a napkin or fairly thick handkerchief.

EFFECT

A handkerchief is spread on the table and four coins are placed near the corners, with the two cards lying along with them. Picking up the cards, you show various ways in which they can be used to cover any two of the coins. After deciding on diagonal corners, you take the uncovered coins, one at a time, under the handkerchief and cause each coin to mysteriously penetrate the cloth under the card at corner A. At the end of the trick, all four coins appear under the card—including the coin at corner D—which you apparently never touched during the entire performance.

METHOD

The presentation depends upon a well-designed routine that directs the spectators' attention away from the few simple moves required. By following it with the actual items, all the details can be easily learned and mastered.

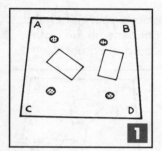

1 Begin by laying out four coins, one on each corner of the cloth, as shown. The cards are tossed on the handkerchief as you say, "Here are four coins, two cards, and one handkerchief."

2 Pick up a card in each hand, thumb on top, fingers below, and cover the two coins at corners C and D. Say, "I can use these cards to cover the two coins in this row."

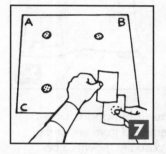

3 Lift the cards and move them to cover the coins at corners A and B. Say, "Or I can cover the coins in this row."

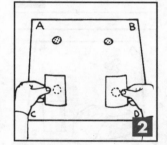

4 Your right hand moves again to cover the coin at D, while your left hand moves its card from A across to B. State, "Also, I can cover two coins at the sides."

5 As you cover the coin at D, your right thumb presses down on the left edge of the coin so that the fingers of your right hand can slide under the coin and secretly pick it up and hold it against the card.

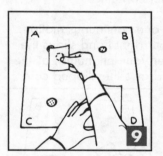

6 When you secretly pick up the coin, it is important that your right fingers make as little motion as possible. Your right hand should look completely natural, with no suspicious movements that might give you away. Also, you will find the pick-up much easier to do if you are performing on a soft surface, such as a rubber mat.

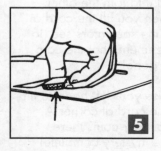

7 Your left hand draws its card toward you, sliding it over the right-hand card, as if to cover the coin at corner D.

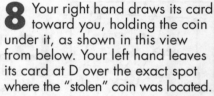

8 Your right hand draws its card toward you, holding the coin under it, as shown in this view from below. Your left hand leaves its card at D over the exact spot where the "stolen" coin was located.

9 Your right hand then places its card over the coin at corner A, leaving with it the coin that it secretly brought from D. Leave the cards at A and D as you comment, "Or I can cover two coins, 'crisscross,' like this."

10 The buildup and timing are important. By covering C-D, then A-B, then B-D, you condition the spectators to expect another simple placement of cards. The fact that the left hand is moved first, showing the coin at B, will cause people to think they also saw the coin at D before the left-hand card covered it.

11 Remark that you have now covered coins at the diagonal corners (A and D). Pick up the coin from C with your right hand and lift that corner of the cloth with your left hand, as shown. State that you will now magically push the coin up through the cloth, causing it to join the coin under the card at corner A.

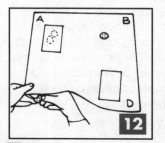

12 Here you make another secret move. As you remove your right hand under the cloth, secretly clip the coin between the tips of the fingers of your left hand. Your right hand should continue its forward motion under the cloth as you secretly transfer the coin from your right to your left hand.

13 The secret transfer of the coin is shown from a different view here.

14 When the now-empty right hand is under the coins at corner A, make a slight upward flicking movement with the right fingers, causing the coins under the card to clink together. Explain that the coin has just penetrated the cloth and joined the coin under the card.

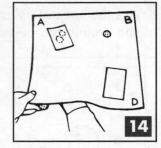

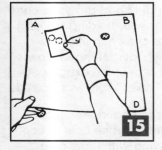

15 The right hand is now removed from under the cloth and casually shown to be empty, as it reaches to turn over the card at corner A. The left fingers still hold the clipped coin, but they keep it hidden beneath the handkerchief.

16 The right hand turns over the card at corner A, and in the same motion moves the card toward your left hand, bringing it directly over corner C.

17 In one continuous motion, your right hand slides the card under your left thumb, as the left hand draws the clipped coin from under the cloth, pressing it up against the card.

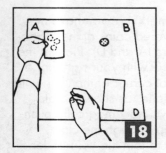

18 The left hand places the card over the two coins at corner A, secretly adding the coin it holds under the card.

19 Your left hand returns to corner C and lifts the cloth, while your right hand picks up the coin at corner B. Announce that you will push another coin up through the cloth.

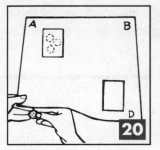

20 Place your right hand under the cloth the same as before, with your left fingers clipping the coin and stealing it away as your right hand goes beneath the cloth.

21 The right hand then pretends to push the coin up through the cloth under the card at corner A (also with a clink).

22 Remove your right hand from beneath the cloth and lift the card at corner A.

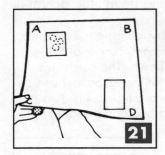

23 As you reveal the three coins, turn the card over toward your left hand, which has the clipped coin ready. Remark, "And another coin has come up through!"

24 As before, the right hand transfers the card to the left hand, which secretly carries the coin away beneath the card. Place the card over the three coins at corner A, just as before, secretly adding the fourth coin.

NOTE: Be careful not to let the secret coin clink against the other coins as you lay the card down.

25 With no more coins in view, you remind the spectators that one coin is still under the other card at corner D. Command it to join the other three. When you lift the card at corner D, the spectators see, to their amazement, that the coin has really gone!

26 Use your left hand to lift the card at corner A, showing all four coins there, making the mystery complete!

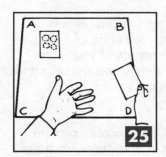

COMMENTS AND SUGGESTIONS

The entire routine should be practiced until it can be done smoothly and without hesitation, especially where the secret moves are concerned. You may experiment with other patterns of covering the coins that work well in directing attention away from the right hand when it secretly picks up the coin at corner D. For example, cover the coins at A and B, then bring the right-hand card down to D, so that A and D are covered. Now the left hand moves its card from A to B, while your right fingers secretly pick up the coin at D. All attention is naturally centered on the left-hand card. From there, simply proceed with the usual routine. Watch the reactions of the spectators whenever you present this excellent close-up mystery, and other ideas will suggest themselves.

FINGER-PALM VANISH

EFFECT

The FINGER-PALM VANISH is an important sleight to master. In this vanish, a coin is retained in the same spot in your left hand from start to finish. This allows you to perform the sleight either swiftly or slowly, as you prefer. You will need to learn this trick in order to perform many MONEY MAGIC tricks.

METHOD
The illustrations on the left are the magician's view and on the right the spectators' view.

1 Display a coin lying on the fingers of your right hand, as shown.

3 The right hand starts to turn over toward you. At the same time, curl your right fingers inward just enough to hold the coin securely in the right fingers, as shown. The coin is now in the finger-palm position.

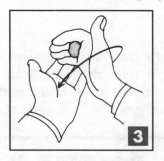
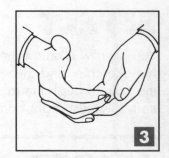

2 Your left hand is held palm up, about waist high, with your left fingers pointing just to the right of the center of the spectators. The little finger of your right hand rests across the tips of your left fingers.

4 Tip your right hand over even more. This is the moment when the coin should be falling into your left hand. Actually, the right hand secretly retains the coin in the finger-palm position.

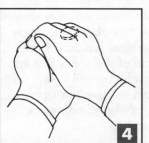
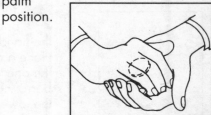

5 Your left fingers close, as if they contained the coin. Your right hand begins to move away from your left hand with the coin secretly finger-palmed.

 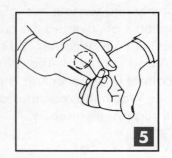

7 Lower your right hand casually to your side as your eyes follow your left hand. This is misdirection.

6 As your left hand closes into a loose fist, your right hand pauses briefly, pointing the first finger toward the closed left hand, which carries attention away to the left.

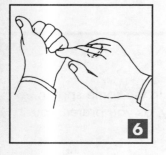 

8 The left hand is now on its own. It apparently squeezes the coin into nothing and opens to show that the coin has vanished.

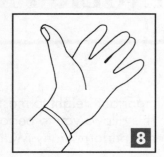 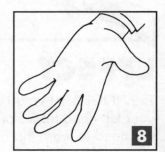

COIN-VANISHING HANDKERCHIEF I

EFFECT

You borrow a coin from a spectator and have it marked for future identification. You place the coin under a pocket handkerchief and give it to another spectator to hold. Under these conditions, even though the spectator can feel the coin through the fabric of the handkerchief and the audience can plainly see its shape, you cause the marked coin to vanish right from under the spectator's fingertips!

SECRET AND PREPARATION

The following method for the vanish of a coin or any other small object has many uses.

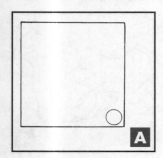

A You will need an inexpensive pocket handkerchief. Place the handkerchief flat on a table. Place a coin of the same size as the one which you will later borrow from the spectator on the lower right-hand corner of the handkerchief.

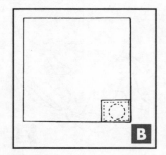

B Cover the coin with a small, square piece of matching fabric (a piece cut from a duplicate handkerchief is perfect). Sew the four edges of the small square of cloth to the handkerchief. The coin is now hidden inside a secret pocket you have made in the corner of the handkerchief.

METHOD

1 Put the prepared handkerchief into your pocket or lay it on your table. If you can do so, it's a nice touch to wear it as a part of your wardrobe. If worn in your topcoat pocket, as an example, it subtly influences the spectators into assuming that the handkerchief is not a magical prop.

2 Borrow a coin from a spectator that duplicates the coin hidden in your handkerchief. Bring the spectator up on the platform with you and have the spectator mark the coin for identification. Stand the spectator to your left and remove your pocket handkerchief.

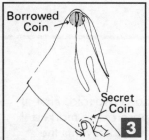

3 Hold the borrowed coin between your left thumb and first fingers, with your fingers and thumb pointing up and one side of the coin pointing toward the spectators. With your right hand, cover the coin and your left hand with the prepared handkerchief. The corner with the secret pocket should be on the side of the handkerchief that is toward you, as shown.

4 Grasp the hidden coin with the right thumb and fingers and, with your right hand, lift the corner with the concealed duplicate coin up under the handkerchief. Position it next to the borrowed coin.

5 At this point, you substitute the hidden coin for the marked coin by palming the marked coin in your left hand. Withdraw your left hand, holding the borrowed coin, as shown.

NOTE: Either your right or your left hand can be used for palming and removing the borrowed coin. Use whichever hand is easier for you and whichever works best for producing the coin at the end. In the illustrations, your left hand is shown palming the spectator's coin, while your right hand holds the handkerchief and the secret, duplicate coin.

6 Grasp the secret coin through the fabric of the handkerchief with your left hand. Remove your right hand from beneath the handkerchief as you hold the coin with your left thumb and fingers. With your right hand, twist the cloth around below the coin. Make sure that the audience doesn't get a flash of the marked coin that is palmed in your left hand.

7 Grasp the handkerchief beneath the coin with your right hand and offer the cloth-covered coin to a spectator to hold. Act naturally, and remember that the audience's attention is on the duplicate coin which is now under the handkerchief. Ask the spectator to hold the coin through the fabric of the handkerchief as you either casually drop the marked coin into your pocket or place it in position for its mysterious reappearance.

8 When you are ready for the vanish, ask the spectator if the coin can still be felt under the handkerchief. Of course, the spectator will reply, "Yes."

9 Grasp one corner of the handkerchief and jerk the handkerchief and the coin away from the spectator's grasp. It will appear as if the coin has vanished from the spectator's fingertips.

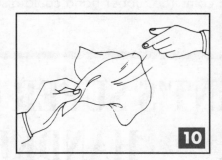

10 Casually show the handkerchief on both sides and replace it in your pocket. You may now reproduce the borrowed coin in any manner you wish.

COIN-VANISHING HANDKERCHIEF II

EFFECT

The effect is the same as COIN-VANISHING HANDKERCHIEF I except that in this case the borrowed coin is further secured in the handkerchief by a rubber band before the vanish.

SECRET AND PREPARATION

In addition to the specially prepared handkerchief, you will need a small rubber band, which you place in your left coat pocket.

METHOD

1 Proceed with COIN-VANISHING HANDKERCHIEF I through Step 7.

2 As the left hand leaves with the palmed marked coin, reach into your coat pocket and remove the rubber band, leaving the coin in your pocket.

3 Place the rubber band around the handkerchief below the coin, as shown.

NOTE: The reason for the rubber band is two-fold. First, it permits a natural way in which to dispose of the marked coin in your pocket temporarily. Second, it prevents the spectator from visually inspecting the contents of the handkerchief while the spectator is holding the coin.

4 When you are ready for the vanish, ask the spectator to be sure the coin is still there. After the spectator says that it is, remove the rubber band. Quickly snap the handkerchief out of the spectator's hand as usual.

COMMENTS AND SUGGESTIONS

The addition of the rubber band can come in handy to cover what might otherwise be a suspicious move when you pocket the borrowed coin. The rubber band could also be placed in the location from which the marked coin will reappear.

GRANT'S SUPER COIN-VANISHING HANDKERCHIEF

"Gen" Grant

Here is a clever variation of the COIN-VANISHING HANDKERCHIEF. The construction of this handkerchief is different in that the secret coin, which is concealed in the corner of the handkerchief, is removable. Therefore, the handkerchief can be adapted to many different tricks requiring the vanish of various-sized coins or other small objects.

METHOD

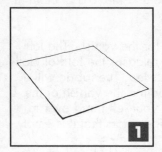

1 Purchase two identical pocket handkerchiefs. Open up one of them on your table, as shown.

2 Cut a 2" square from the corner of the second handkerchief and place it over the matching corner of the first handkerchief.

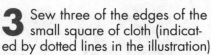

3 Sew three of the edges of the small square of cloth (indicated by dotted lines in the illustration) to the first handkerchief. Leave the outside seam, A to D, open.

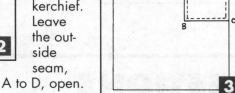

NOTE: The unhemmed edges of the corner patch, A to B and B to C, should be turned under before sewing to prevent the cut edges from fraying.

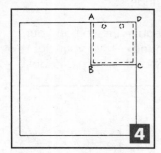

4 Sew two small dress snaps on the inside hem of the open seam (A to D), as indicated. You now have a secret pocket in the corner of the handkerchief that will safely conceal a coin or other small object inside.

NOTE: The most important value of this specially prepared handkerchief is that you can insert any coin or small object into the secret pocket. A ring, coin, or folded-up dollar bill are just a few examples of small items that can be vanished with this versatile and inexpensive piece of magical apparatus.

COIN THROUGH LEG

EFFECT

You apparently cause a half-dollar to magically pass completely through your right leg.

METHOD

All that is required are an unprepared half-dollar and mastery of the finger-palm position.

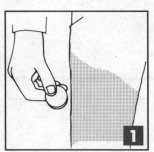

1 Display a half-dollar to the spectators. The coin is held between the thumb and fingers of your right hand. Lower the coin to your right side, next to your right pants leg, slightly above your right knee.

2 Place the coin on your leg, as shown. Your right thumb holds the coin against your pants leg just above the knee.

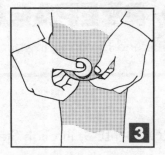

3 Bring your left hand over beside the coin. With the fingers of both the right and left hands, lift a portion of the pants fabric up and under the coin.

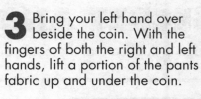

4 Fold the cloth, which you pulled under the coin, up and over the coin. Your left thumb holds the fold of cloth in place.

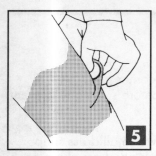

5 This is how the coin and folded cloth should look to you.

6 As soon as the coin is covered by the fold in the pants leg, the thumb of your right hand secretly pulls the coin up behind your right fingers.

7 Finger-palm the coin in your right hand. Move your right hand away and, slowly and deliberately, place it behind your right leg.

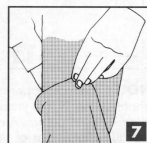

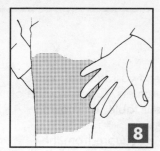

NOTE: Your right hand will appear to be empty, while your left hand is apparently still holding the coin behind the fold of cloth in your pants leg.

8 Now for the vanish. The left hand releases the fold of cloth in the pants leg. The fabric will drop, revealing the vanish of the coin. Turn your left hand over to show the spectators that it is empty.

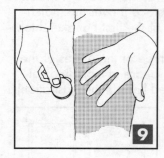

9 With your right hand, slowly withdraw the coin from behind your right knee. Magically, the coin has gone right through your leg!

COMMENTS AND SUGGESTIONS

This is a very clever and easily learned sleight that can be used as a trick in itself as just described; or it can be used for the vanish of a coin, as explained in the next effect, which can be useful in other coin routines.

CHALLENGE COIN VANISH

EFFECT

You display a coin and place it in a fold of cloth on the leg of your pants. A spectator is allowed to feel the coin to see if it is still there. Yet, under these seemingly impossible circumstances, the coin vanishes completely.

SECRET AND PREPARATION

Place a duplicate of the coin you intend to vanish in your right pants pocket.

METHOD

Proceed exactly as in COIN THROUGH LEG, through Step 5.

1 However, when you place the coin that will vanish on your leg in Step 1 this time, position it directly above the secret duplicate coin in your right pants pocket.

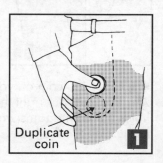

Duplicate coin

NOTE: Because of the location of the duplicate coin in your pocket, it will be necessary to place the vanishing coin slightly higher on your pants leg than in the COIN THROUGH LEG.

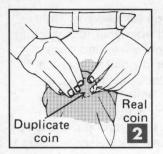

2 When you fold the cloth up around the coin, make sure that the duplicate coin is in the fold of cloth on top of the coin that will vanish.

3 You now have the real coin, the one that the spectators know about, under the duplicate coin, which is really in your right pants pocket.

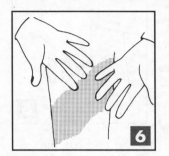

4 Proceed to "steal" the coin away in the finger-palm position as explained in Step 7 in COIN THROUGH LEG.

5 Ask a spectator to feel and see if the coin is still there. The spectator will feel the duplicate coin, which is in your pocket. This gives you ideal misdirection to secretly drop the finger-palmed coin into your right coat pocket.

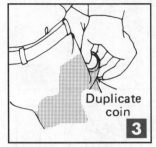

6 After the spectator is satisfied that the coin is still there, merely let the fold of cloth drop, as before. You may then show both hands to be completely empty. The coin has vanished.

COIN À GO-GO

EFFECT

You borrow a half-dollar from a spectator. The spectator is handed a pencil with which to mark the coin. Working at very close range, you cause the coin to vanish right before the spectator's eyes, utilizing the pencil and an impromptu wand. You show both hands to be unmistakably empty, and you even hand the pencil to the spectator to examine. Then, to bring the mystery to a happy conclusion, you simply tap the back of the spectator's left hand with the pencil and magically reproduce the marked coin.

SECRET AND PREPARATION

This is a very good impromptu trick. Carry a marking pen, ballpoint pen, or just a regular lead pencil in your left inside coat pocket, and you are always ready to perform. To insure the proper working of the effect, do not use a coin smaller than a quarter. Only one sleight is used, the FINGER-PALM VANISH (see page 47). After you have mastered this move, this routine will become an excellent addition to your impromptu program.

METHOD

3 Toss the coin from hand . . .   **4** . . . to hand . . .

1 Borrow a half-dollar from a spectator and have the spectator mark it with the pen or pencil. Let's suppose you are using a pencil. After the spectator is satisfied that the coin can be identified later, replace the pencil in your left-hand inside coat pocket.

2 Place the coin in the palm of your right hand.

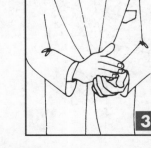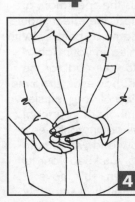

5 . . . finally ending up with the half-dollar enclosed in your left hand.

6 Reach into your inside coat pocket with your right hand and retrieve the pencil.

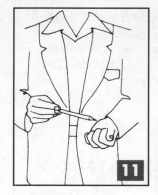

7 Point the pencil at your left hand and ask the spectator to call, "Heads or tails."

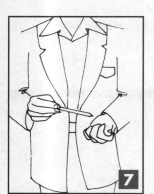

8 After the spectator makes a choice, open your left hand and allow the spectator to verify whether the choice was correct.

NOTE: All of the preceding has nothing to do with the actual working of the trick, but it has added greatly to the misdirection, as you will see.

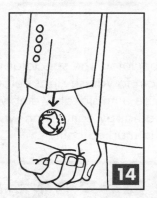

9 Tell the spectator that you would like to try it again. Replace the pencil in your pocket and once again toss the coin back and forth from hand to hand. However, on the last toss, when you apparently throw the coin into your left hand, execute the FINGER-PALM VANISH with your right hand. Secretly retain the coin in your right hand as your left hand apparently closes over the coin.

10 As far as the spectators are concerned, the effect should be exactly the same as before. With the coin concealed in your right hand, reach into your coat for the pencil. This time, however, drop the coin down the top of your left sleeve at the inside armhole of your coat. The coin will fall down your sleeve to your left elbow and will remain there as long as you keep your left arm bent, as shown. This move should be accomplished smoothly.

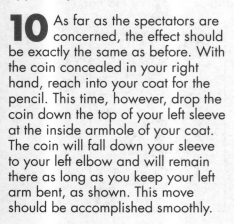

11 As you remove your right hand from your jacket, bring the pencil into view, and once again use it to point to your left hand. Ask the spectator to call, "heads" or "tails." Since every move you have just made duplicates the first run-through, the spectator will have absolutely no reason for doubting the presence of the coin in your left hand.

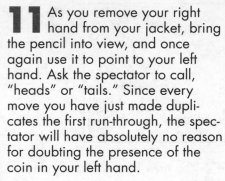

12 After the spectator has made the choice, slowly open the hand and reveal the startling vanish of the coin. Hand the pencil to the spectator and show that both of your hands are completely empty.

13 Lower your left arm to your side, as you ask the spectator to return the pencil.

14 The spectator's eyes will be diverted by the pencil, as the marked coin falls silently into your left palm. Take the pencil back from the spectator, as you close your left hand around the coin.

15 Raise your left hand to waist level and tap it with the pencil.

16 Slowly open your hand, revealing the magical reappearance of the coin. Have the spectator identify the half-dollar as being the original borrowed coin and thank the spectator for assisting you.

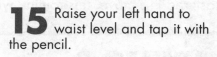

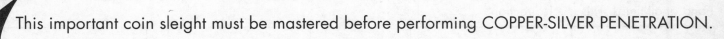

FRENCH DROP

This important coin sleight must be mastered before performing COPPER-SILVER PENETRATION.

METHOD

The illustrations on the left are the magician's view and on the right the spectators' view.

1 Hold a coin so that it is level between the tips of your left thumb and fingers. All four fingers and the thumb of your left hand should point upward. Your fingers should be held closely together so the spectators cannot see between them.

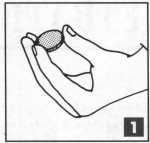

2 Your right hand approaches from behind to apparently take the coin by sliding your right thumb beneath it and your right fingers above the coin. Your left hand should be held so the coin can still be seen.

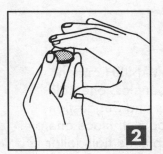
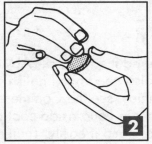

3 The fingers of your right hand close over the coin, covering it, as shown.

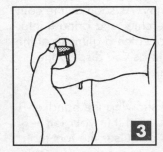

4 As your right hand pauses momentarily, your left thumb releases the coin, so that it secretly drops into the bend of your left fingers.

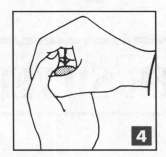

5 Without hesitation, your right hand closes into a fist as if taking the coin from your left fingers.

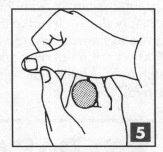

6 In one continuous motion, turn both hands over (see arrows) as you turn your body to the right. Just twist your left hand inward, toward your body, so the coin stays hidden from view; at the same time, turn your right hand so that its closed fingers face the spectators. As you rotate your hands, your left first finger casually points toward your right hand. Follow your right hand with your eyes, as it is supposed to contain the coin.

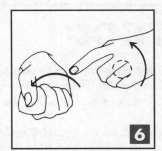

7 As your right hand moves away, casually let your left hand fall to your side with the coin held secretly in its curled fingers. Your eyes should remain fixed on your right hand at all times. This is misdirection.

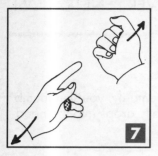 

8 Slowly begin to make a rubbing motion with your right fingers, as if to rub the coin away. Then, open your hand to show the coin has vanished.

 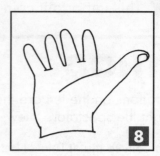

COPPER-SILVER PENETRATION

EFFECT

You request the assistance of a spectator and ask that the spectator stand to your left. You remove two coins from your pants pocket. One of the coins is an English penny; the other is an American half-dollar. Both of these coins are the same size, but the copper penny contrasts with the silver half-dollar. The coins are handed to a spectator for examination. You then display an empty pocket handkerchief and wrap the silver half-dollar in it. The half-dollar, wrapped in the handkerchief, is given to the spectator to hold. You call the spectator's attention to the English penny. You then invisibly throw the penny toward the handkerchief. To everyone's surprise, the vanished penny is heard magically penetrating the handkerchief and falling alongside the half-dollar! The spectator is asked to open out the handkerchief to verify the coin's arrival.

SECRET AND PREPARATION

In order to present this effect, it will be necessary for you to have mastered the FINGER-PALM VANISH and the FRENCH DROP or any other sleight-of-hand vanish of a coin. You will also need two English pennies, one half-dollar, and a pocket handkerchief. (If you do not have two English pennies, see the Comments and Suggestions section at the end of this trick.) Fold the pocket handkerchief and place it in your inside coat pocket. Place one of the English pennies next to the handkerchief, so that you will be able to grasp it easily. Then, put the half-dollar and the duplicate English penny into your right pants pocket.

METHOD

1 Ask for the assistance of a spectator and have this person stand to your left. (This will give you the most protection from accidental exposure during the presentation.)

2 Remove the penny and the half-dollar from your right pants pocket and give them to the spectator for examination.

3 While the spectator is busy examining the coins, reach into your inside coat pocket with your left hand and secretly finger-palm the duplicate penny. As soon as the coin is securely palmed, grasp the handkerchief and bring it into view. Make sure the spectators do not catch a glimpse of the hidden coin as you display the handkerchief.

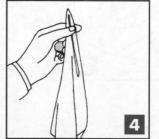

4 After showing the handkerchief, hold it in your left hand. This disguises the fact that you are also concealing a coin in that hand.

5 Ask the spectator for the half-dollar. Hold the coin by your right fingertips and display it to the spectators. Transfer the half-dollar, so that it is held by your left fingertips. Your left hand is now holding the half-dollar in plain view, the duplicate copper penny in a finger-palm, and a corner of the handkerchief. The illustration shows the positions of the three objects.

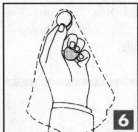

6 Your right hand grasps the bottom corner of the handkerchief and snaps it free of your left hand. Cover your left hand and the coin(s) with the handkerchief.

NOTE: Position the handkerchief so that the half-dollar is near the center of the handkerchief.

7 With your right fingers, grasp the half-dollar through the fabric and lift the coin out of your left fingers.

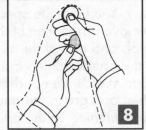

8 Under cover of the handkerchief, with your left hand, secretly place the finger-palmed penny into the palm of your right hand. The English penny stays under the handkerchief as your right fingers curl around the handkerchief and the penny and hold the penny through the fabric under the handkerchief, as shown.

9 Have the spectator grasp the half-dollar through the fabric of the handkerchief. As the spectator does this, slide the penny down, inside the handkerchief, as you continue to hold the penny with your right fingers.

10 Turn the handkerchief parallel to the floor. Slide your right hand to the right end of the handkerchief (where the corners are). As you slide your hand, leave the penny in the middle area, as shown. The penny is now in the handkerchief between your right hand and the spectator's hand holding the half-dollar.

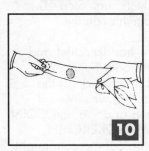

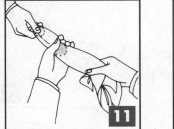

11 Immediately reach up with your left hand and hold the

penny in place by grasping the handkerchief in the middle, as shown.

12 Ask the spectator to hold the handkerchief with a free hand somewhere between your right and left hands, as shown.

NOTE: Since the duplicate penny is being held by your left hand, the spectator cannot accidentally feel the penny.

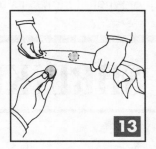

13 You can now remove your hands from the handkerchief. As long as the spectator's hands are held apart and the handkerchief is kept level with the floor, the hidden penny will stay in place. Pick up the visible penny and display it in your left hand.

14 Reach over with your right hand and execute the FRENCH DROP. As you know, the move will lead the spectators to believe that the penny is in your closed right hand, when actually it is secretly being held in your left hand. (If you prefer, any other vanishing sleight may be used here.)

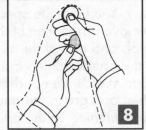

15 Move your right hand, supposedly containing the penny, above the handkerchief being held by the spectator. You are about to slap the handkerchief free of the spectator's right hand. To accomplish this correctly, be sure to strike the handkerchief as close to the half-dollar as possible. Make a sharp downward motion with your right hand. Open your hand just before it hits the handkerchief.

16 The handkerchief will fall free of the spectator's right hand, causing the hidden copper coin to fall into the center of the handkerchief and strike the half-dollar. It appears that the penny penetrated the handkerchief and joined the half-dollar.

17 The spectator is told to unfold the handkerchief. Both coins will be discovered in its center. While the spectator is examining the coins, secretly drop the duplicate penny into your pocket.

COMMENTS AND SUGGESTIONS

This is an excellent sleight-of-hand trick. Although it requires a bit of practice to get all of the moves and the timing correct, it is well worth the effort. If you do not have two English pennies, you may substitute any two heavy coins. Foreign coins are best since you can get more contrast between the coins. However, two American coins may be used as well: for instance, one half-dollar and two quarters, or one silver dollar and two half-dollars. In this case, it is better to use the smaller as the duplicate coin, as these are the two that are involved in all of the palming. The different sizes will not matter since the spectator feels only one coin (the larger coin) when he holds the coin under the handkerchief. Thus the difference in size will not be noticed. Just be sure that the duplicate coin is heavy enough to fall within the handkerchief when it makes its mysterious appearance with the other coin.

SHRINKING COIN

EFFECT

You borrow a finger ring from one spectator and a half-dollar from another. You also request that these two spectators assist you on stage as you present your next mystery. You have the spectators stand beside you, one spectator on your left side and the other on your right. You remove a handkerchief from your pocket. The borrowed half-dollar is wrapped secretly in the center of the handkerchief, and one of the spectators threads the four corners of the handkerchief through the ring, imprisoning the coin in the handkerchief. Each of the spectators is asked to hold two corners of the handkerchief (one in each hand) and to stretch the handkerchief out between them so that it is parallel to the floor. You reach underneath the handkerchief and grasp the ring and the imprisoned coin. You then ask the spectators to gently pull on the corners of the handkerchief. To the amazement of all, the coin slowly penetrates up through the ring. The ring is now free. You remove it from under the handkerchief, and the coin lies on the handkerchief held between the two spectators. All of the items can be examined. The ring and coin are returned to the spectators, along with your thanks for their assistance.

SECRET AND PREPARATION

All that is required for this effect is a pocket handkerchief, a half-dollar, and a finger ring, all of which are quite ordinary. You must also be able to perform the COIN THROUGH HANDKERCHIEF trick. No preparation is necessary because this is a completely impromptu mystery.

METHOD

1 Borrow a half-dollar and a finger ring from spectators. You will also need the assistance of two spectators. If they are the same ones who lent you the borrowed articles, so much the better.

2 Remove your pocket handkerchief and display the borrowed half-dollar. Wrap the coin in the center of the handkerchief as described in COIN THROUGH HANDKERCHIEF (see page 40). As you know, the special way in which you wrap the coin leaves the coin on the outside of the handkerchief. To the spectators, it appears as though the coin is actually held inside the handkerchief. Follow the COIN THROUGH HANDKERCHIEF routine only through Step 10. Do not perform the penetration of the coin through the handkerchief.

3 Hold the handkerchief and coin with both hands, as shown. Be sure the side of the handkerchief that was toward you in Steps 8 and 9 of the COIN THROUGH HANDKERCHIEF, where a portion of the coin might be visible, is resting next to your left fingers, so the spectators cannot see that the coin is not really inside the handkerchief.

4 Have the spectator thread the four corners of the handkerchief through the ring, as shown. As the spectator does this, retain your grip on the coin with your left hand. Also hold the handkerchief above the coin with your right hand, as shown, so the handkerchief does not untwist, revealing the coin.

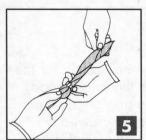

5 After the spectator has threaded the ends through the ring, tell the spectator to slide the ring down the handkerchief until it rests tightly against the wrapped coin. This will lock the coin into position and keep the handkerchief from unwrapping.

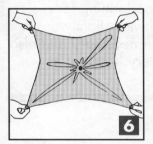

6 Ask the spectators to hold the four corners of the handkerchief, as shown. The handkerchief should be level with the floor. The coin and ring are hanging underneath the handkerchief.

NOTE: To the spectators, it appears that you have placed the borrowed coin underneath the handkerchief. Then a spectator has threaded the ring over the corners of the handkerchief, imprisoning the coin in the center. Since the coin is much larger than the inside of the ring, there is apparently no way for the coin to escape.

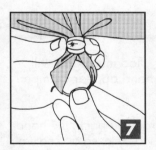

7 Using both hands, reach underneath the outstretched handkerchief. Grasp the ring with the thumb and first finger of your left hand. Work the ring slightly upward so that you gain a bit of slack in the handkerchief. With the right hand you can now slip the coin free of the handkerchief, as shown.

8 It is important to remember that from now until the coin penetrates the ring in Step 13, you have to hold the center of the handkerchief with your left hand, so that the spectators are not aware that you have removed the coin.

9 Under the handkerchief, secretly finger-palm the coin in your right hand. As your right second and third fingers hold the coin finger-palmed, your right first finger and thumb pull the ring off the handkerchief and place it in your left hand, so that the ring may be held by your left third and fourth fingers, as shown.

NOTE: As pointed out in Step 8, be sure to maintain your grip on the fabric with your left thumb and first finger so that the spectators are unaware that either the coin or the ring has been removed.

10 Bring your right hand with the secretly finger-palmed coin out from beneath the handkerchief. Move your right hand directly over the center of the handkerchief, as shown.

11 The following step is most important. Your right hand secretly drops the coin into the well in the center of the handkerchief (which the spectators think is made by the ring and coin). Under the handkerchief, your left fingers open momentarily to let the coin into the well.

NOTE: The drawing in Step 11 shows the right hand held high above the handkerchief. This is only to illustrate the move. When you are actually performing the trick, your hand should be resting directly on top of the fabric when the drop is made.

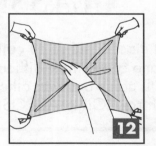

12 When the coin is dropped into the well, the left fingers open to receive it and then close around the coin and the fabric. To the spectators, the handkerchief appears just as it did before. Your right hand continues to move over the handkerchief, apparently smoothing out its folds. This smoothing move is used before and after the drop as misdirection of what you are really doing, which is secretly bringing the coin from beneath the handkerchief and dropping it into the well.

NOTE: At this point, the spectator's borrowed ring is held by your left third and fourth fingers under the handkerchief. The coin is now on top of the handkerchief in the well. Your left thumb and first finger hold the handkerchief closed over the coin, so that all appears as it did at the start.

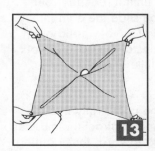

13 As your left hand continues to hold the ring and coin, have the spectators gently pull on the four corners of the handkerchief. With your left fingers, let the coin slowly appear from the well, as it works its way up through your left fingers. To the spectators, it will appear that the coin is passing through the ring, which is much smaller than the coin.

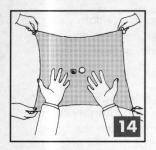

14 When the coin is completely on top of the handkerchief, and the handkerchief is stretched flat between the two spectators, with your left hand slowly and dramatically bring the ring from under the handkerchief. Drop it next to the coin on the outstretched cloth. The effect is two-fold. The coin has passed through the much smaller ring, which also releases the ring from the handkerchief. You may now pass the ring, the coin, and the handkerchief for examination, as you thank the spectators for their assistance.

COMMENTS AND SUGGESTIONS

This is a very clever adaptation of the COIN THROUGH HANDKERCHIEF move. It is particularly misleading for the spectators since the effect is that the coin does not penetrate the handkerchief but passes through the ring instead. The outstretched handkerchief forms a perfect cover when you secretly palm the coin and slip the ring off the handkerchief. This makes an ideal close-up effect since it may be performed at any time and uses small borrowed articles, all of which may be examined. The effect works particularly well if performed so that the handkerchief is held over a low table (such as a coffee table) at which you and the other participants are seated. If performing for a larger group, have the spectators who are holding the handkerchief tilt the side nearest the audience slightly downward so that the handkerchief is angled toward the audience. This will allow you all of the cover necessary and also keep anyone from seeing under the handkerchief as you perform this miniature miraculous mystery.

CLASSIC PALM

This is probably the oldest and most basic of all coin sleights. It is used to conceal a coin in the hand in a natural manner. It is also one of the most difficult to master. However, once learned, it will be of great value to you, not only with coins but with other objects as well. You will need to master the CLASSIC PALM in order to perform COINS ACROSS.

METHOD

1 Place a coin on the tips of your two middle fingers and hold it there with the tip of your thumb.

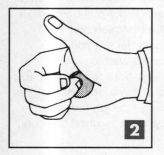

2 Move the thumb and bend your fingertips inward, sliding the coin along the underside of your thumb until it reaches your palm. As you slide the coin into the palm, stretch your hand open so the muscles at the base of your thumb and little finger are fully expanded.

3 Press the coin firmly into the palm and contract the muscles of your hand inward, thus gaining a grip on the edges of the coin. Draw your thumb inward only as far as needed to retain the coin

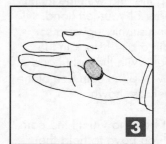

comfortably. Too much grip will make your hand appear cramped and tense.

4 Seen from the back, the hand should look relaxed and natural, with the fingers close together.

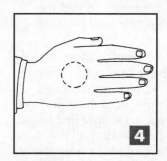

5 Avoid the common fault of holding the coin too tightly and spreading the thumb and fingers wide, as shown here. This will give away the fact that you are hiding something. Only when the hand looks natural will you be above suspicion and thus have mastered the CLASSIC PALM.

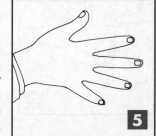

COMMENTS AND SUGGESTIONS

The term "palm" comes from this method of concealment, as the coin is actually gripped in the palm of the hand. Keep practicing until you can place the coin in just the right position. It will then become second nature and will prove extremely useful. Once the knack is acquired, coins of various sizes can be retained. It is a good idea to use the hand containing the palmed coin for various gestures such as snapping the fingers, pulling back the sleeve, or picking up articles from the table. These natural actions will direct attention away from the hand, because people will automatically assume that it is empty.

NOTE: The object being palmed must be placed in the classic-palm position with the aid of only the finger and thumb of the hand doing the palming. There should be no help from your other hand. You should also practice this important sleight so that you can palm objects in either hand with equal ease.

COINS ACROSS

EFFECT

You are seated at a table. From your pocket you remove six coins and place them on the table, arranging them in two rows of three coins each. You gather three coins into each hand and magically cause the three coins from your right hand to travel, one at a time, to your left hand.

SECRET AND PREPARATION

In order to present this classic sleight-of-hand effect, you must first have learned the CLASSIC PALM. Since this mystery is presented as a close-up trick, you should practice until you can perform the CLASSIC PALM easily. You also will need seven identical coins. Be sure to pick coins that are easy for you to palm. Use quarters, half-dollars, or silver dollars, depending on the size of your hands. Place the seven coins in your right pocket.

METHOD

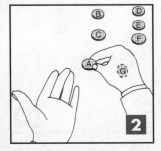

1 Reach into your pocket and remove the coins. As you do, secretly palm one of the coins. Arrange the six remaining coins on the table in two rows of three, as shown. In the illustrations, we have lettered the six coins on the table A, B, C, D, E, and F, and the seventh palmed coin, as G.

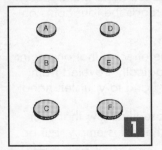

2 With your right hand concealing the seventh coin, G, reach across the table and pick up the first coin, A, from the left row.

3 If the angles permit (that is, if the spectators are located in front of you), you may now dis-

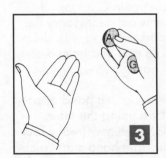

play coin A at the tips of your thumb and fingers of the right hand while still concealing the palmed coin, G, as shown here. The fingers and thumb of the right hand point up, and the palmed coin is concealed from the spectators. If, on the other hand, you are surrounded by the spectators, just keep your right hand with your palm toward the table, as you place the coins into your left hand.

4 Throw this first coin, A, into your open left hand.

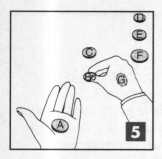

5 With your right hand still concealing coin G, reach across the table and pick up the second coin, B, from the left-hand row.

6 Throw coin B into your open left hand alongside coin A.

7 The right hand picks up the third and last coin, C, in the left-hand row. Coin G is still hidden in your right palm.

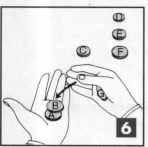

NOTE: Watch your angles to be sure that you do

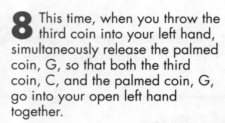

not flash the palmed coin, G, during Steps 1 through 7.

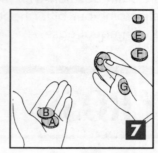

8 This time, when you throw the third coin into your left hand, simultaneously release the palmed coin, G, so that both the third coin, C, and the palmed coin, G, go into your open left hand together.

9 Close your left hand immediately around the four coins and turn your hand over. At this point, the spectators believe that you simply counted three coins into your left hand.

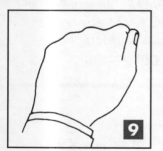

NOTE: Although the illustration in Step 8 shows coin C on top of coin G, this is not necessarily the way the coins will land. Just drop both coins as one and immediately close your hand.

10 With your left hand apparently holding the three coins from the left row (really four coins), your right hand starts picking up the three coins (D, E, and F) still on the table.

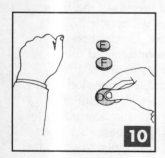

11 Pick up the first coin, D, and display it in your right hand. As you do, position the coin in your hand in readiness for the CLASSIC PALM.

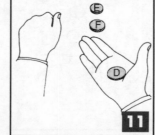

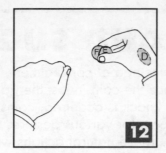

12 Close your right hand and turn it over. Use your fingers to push coin D into the classic-palm position. Pick up the two remaining coins (E and F) with your thumb and fingers. Close your right fingers around all of the coins.

13 Make sure to keep the palmed coin, D, separated from the last two coins (E and F).

NOTE: At this point, the spectators will believe that each hand contains three coins.

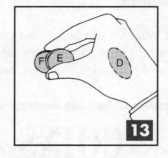

14 Make a slight throwing motion with your right hand in the direction of your left hand. Loosen your left fingers so that the coins in your left hand will clank together. Tell the spectators that one of the coins has magically traveled to your left hand.

15 The right hand retains coin D in the classic-palm position.

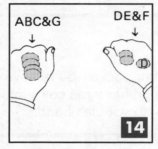

ABC&G   DE&F

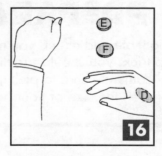

16 At the same time, the right hand places the other two coins (E and F) on the table.

17 The left hand immediately spreads the four coins on the table.

18 The effect is that one coin magically traveled from your right hand to your left hand.

19 Casually show that your left hand is empty, but be sure the spectators are not aware of coin D hidden in your right hand.

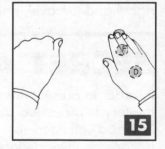

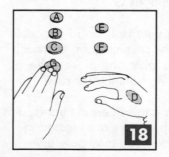

20 You have just learned the basic sequences in creating this effect. From this point on, the basic moves are repeated, from Step 2 through Step 9.

21 The right hand picks up the four coins from the left row one at a time and throws them into your open left hand. As you throw the last coin, G, the palmed coin, D, is added to the other four coins in the left hand.

22 The right hand picks up the two remaining coins on the table. The first coin, E, is placed in the classic-palm position. Be sure to keep the second coin, F, separated from the first coin, E, as in Steps 12 and 13.

23 Make the throwing motion with your right hand. Clink the coins in your left hand to signal the mysterious arrival of the fifth coin.

24 The right hand places only one coin, E, on the table, keeping the other coin, F, in the classic-palm position. The left hand then spreads the five coins on the table.

25 Repeat Steps 2 through 9 as you place the five coins into your left hand. Secretly add the palmed coin, E, from your right hand on the fifth throw.

26 At this point, you will be left with one coin on the table. For this you use a special method of LAPPING

LAPPING—PULL-OFF METHOD

EFFECT

You pick up a coin from the table and it vanishes completely from your hand!

SECRET AND PREPARATION

The following vanish describes how this useful sleight is used for the magical transposition of the last coin in COINS ACROSS.

METHOD

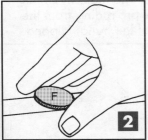

1 Cover the last coin with your right-hand fingers and slide it toward yourself, as if you were going to scoop it up into your hand.

2 Instead of actually picking up the coin . . .

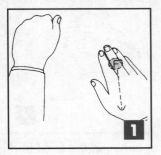

3 . . . allow the coin to fall unseen off the back edge of the table onto your lap, as your right hand continues the scooping motion

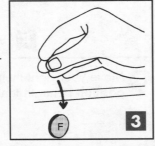

with the fingers apparently closing around the coin.

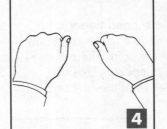

4 Hold both hands closed on the table in front of you.

5 Lift your right hand above your left and apparently rub the coin through the back of your left hand. Show that your right hand is empty.

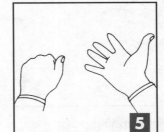

6 Dramatically spread the six coins on the table.

7 While the spectators are examining the six coins, casually retrieve the extra coin from your lap. Add this coin to the six on the table as you gather them up to put them away, or secretly drop it in your coat pocket as you continue your routine.

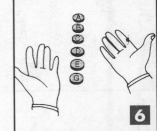

COIN ROLL

Though this is strictly an ornamental flourish and not a magical effect, it belongs in every coin manipulator's program. When you are doing coin tricks, it is always wise to impress the spectators with your skill, causing them to believe that the simplest of your routines must depend upon your remarkable dexterity.

EFFECT

You demonstrate your dexterity as a magician by causing a half-dollar to roll from finger to finger across the back of your hand. When it has finished this surprising run, it drops from sight beneath your little finger and pops up again between the thumb and first finger, only to repeat its remarkable roll. You do this repeatedly, so that the coin really seems to come alive, rolling of its own accord. When you perform the COIN ROLL deftly, it will dress up your coin routine, giving the appearance of great professional dexterity.

METHOD

NOTE: So that you can follow the coin as it rolls over the fingers, we have added the letters A and B to the opposite edges of the coin.

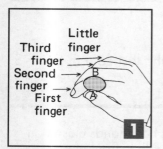

1 Hold the coin by edge A in your right hand between your thumb and first finger, as shown.

2 Push the coin up and release the thumb, allowing the coin to roll over the back of the first finger near the knuckles.

3 Lift the second finger and allow it to clip the right-hand edge B of the coin. The coin will assume a temporary position clipped between the first and second fingers.

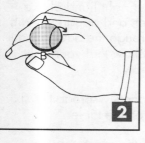

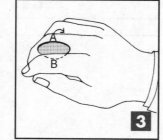

4 Without stopping, raise the first finger, which pushes the coin onto the back of the second finger.

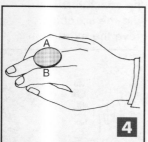

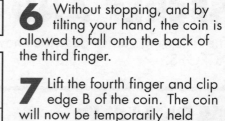

5 Lift the third finger and grip edge A, which allows the coin to roll over the second finger. The coin will again assume a temporary clipped position between the second and third fingers.

6 Without stopping, and by tilting your hand, the coin is allowed to fall onto the back of the third finger.

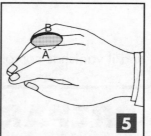

7 Lift the fourth finger and clip edge B of the coin. The coin will now be temporarily held between the third and fourth fingers.

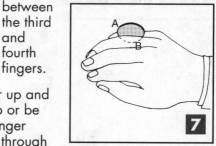

8 Move your little finger up and allow the coin to drop or be pulled down by the little finger through the opening between the third and little fingers. The majority of the coin is now protruding from the palm side of the hand, clipped between the third and little fingers.

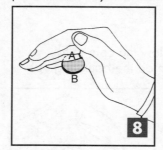

9 Move your right thumb to a position beneath the coin.

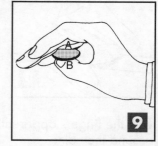

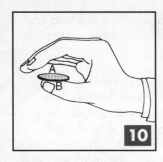

10 Release the coin and balance it on the ball of your right thumb.

11 Move your thumb under your fingers and transfer the coin back to the original starting point at the base of the first finger.

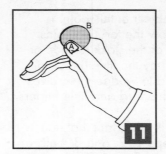

12 You can push the coin up over the knuckle of the first finger and begin the entire sequence again. You may repeat the same set of moves as many times as you wish.

COMMENTS AND SUGGESTIONS

Along with its value as a flourish, the COIN ROLL is very helpful in developing skill in sleight-of-hand, as it loosens up your fingers so they can execute difficult moves with speed and precision.

It will require considerable practice on your part in order to master the COIN ROLL. Depending on the size of your hand, you may wish to use either a quarter or a silver dollar instead of a half-dollar. Also, although all of the moves are described in detail above, you may develop a slightly different technique that is better for your hand. Some performers, through a great deal of practice, are able to roll more than one coin on the same hand, or to roll one coin on the left hand and another on the right hand at the same time. But don't expect to master either of these variations quickly. One great advantage of this type of flourish, however, is that although it requires a great deal of practice, you may practice it while you are doing something else, such as watching television, listening to the radio, or even traveling. You can practice it at any time when your hands are free, and when you will not disturb anyone if you drop the coin, which you surely will as you learn this flourish. Once learned, it is a great attention-getter as you idly sit rolling a coin back, up, and around your fingers!

ROLL DOWN

EFFECT

You display a stack of four coins. Suddenly, the coins ROLL DOWN your fingers, until each coin is held separately between the fingers of your hand.

The ROLL DOWN might be classified as a master flourish. Once learned, it can truly demonstrate your skill as a manipulator. We recommend the use of half-dollars (or silver dollars if you can manage them) for two reasons: The flourish with larger coins appears to be more difficult (in truth it is easier), and a larger group of spectators can see the effect.

METHOD

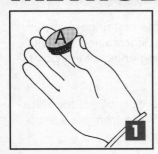

1 Begin by placing four stacked coins in your right hand, holding them between your thumb and first finger. The palm of your right hand should be up, as shown.

2 Bend your second finger into your palm and tilt your hand slightly to the left.

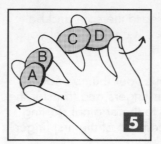

3 The object at this point is to allow the top two coins (A and B) of the stack to slide or be rotated by the little finger to the left and to wedge themselves between the third and little fingers.

NOTE: It is important that you master Steps 1, 2, and 3, before moving on to Step 4. The security with which coins A and B are held between the third and fourth fingers will determine the success or failure of the next steps.

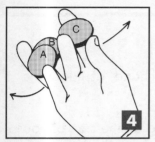

4 With coins A and B held between your third and fourth fingers, lift your second finger and

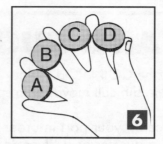

grip the edges of coin B and coin C. Your thumb applies pressure to coin D.

5 Slowly straighten out your fingers. Your thumb pivots coin D to the right, as your little finger pivots coin A to the left. The second finger rolls in between coins B and C, holding their edges.

6 The coins are now in position, dramatically displayed between your fingers.

COMMENTS AND SUGGESTIONS

If you have followed each of the above steps with the four coins in your hand, you will have discovered that this is not an easy flourish to learn. But, with practice, it can be mastered. The obvious display of skill will be instantly recognized and appreciated.

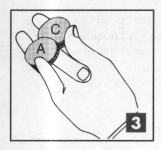

ROLL THE BILLS

For a close-up mystery, this is a real puzzler. It's a good one to perform when someone asks you to do a trick and you're not really prepared.

EFFECT

You lay two bills on the table, say a one-dollar bill and a five-dollar bill, so that they form a V shape. With the one on top, you call attention to the fact that the one-dollar bill is on top of the five. You then begin rolling the two bills together, starting at the point of the V. While you are rolling the bills, you ask a spectator to place a finger on the corner of the one-dollar bill and another finger on the corner of the five. The spectator now has both bills pinned to the table. So far, so good—with no chance for deception. But now, when you unroll the bills, the five is on top of the one, yet the spectator still has a finger on each bill.

METHOD

1 Lay the two bills on the table with the one-dollar bill on top of the five, as shown. Notice that the one is a bit further forward (toward the spectators) than the five. (This illustration is from your viewpoint.)

2 With the first fingers of both hands, start rolling the bills together, beginning at the point of the V.

NOTE: The illustrations for Steps 2 through 9 are from the spectators' viewpoint.

3 Continue rolling the two bills until just a small part of the corner of the five-dollar bill remains in view, then stop. As shown, more of the corner of the one shows, because it was placed further forward in the initial layout (Step 1).

4 The secret move occurs in Steps 4 and 5. As you continue to roll the bills forward, open the fingers of your left hand over the corner of the five. Apparently you are merely holding the bills as you roll them, but actually you are hiding the corner of the five from the spectators' view, as shown. At the same time, point to the corner of the one with your right hand. Ask a spectator to place a finger on that corner to hold it in place.

5 As the spectator does this, place your right finger on the center of the roll of bills and roll them slightly forward. The corner of the five, which is hidden by your left fingers, flops over. In other words, this corner goes beneath the rolled bills and does a forward flip-over back to its original position on the table. This is unknown to the spectators, as it is hidden by your left hand.

6 This is a view of the action as shown from the side. Notice how your left fingers cover the secret flip-over of the corner of the five.

7 Still holding the roll of bills with your right finger, lift your left hand and point to the corner of the five.

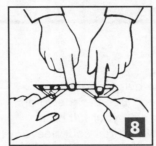

8 Ask the spectator to place a finger on the corner of the five. Emphasize that the spectator is pinning the corners of both bills to the table.

9 All that is left is for you to unroll the bills, as shown. As a result of the secret flip-over of the corner of the five, the position of the bills will be reversed—with the five-dollar bill now on top of the one-dollar bill!

COMMENTS AND SUGGESTIONS

It is not necessary to use bills of different values in order to perform ROLL THE BILLS. If the two bills are the same, simply turn one of them over and you have bills of different colors (one black and one green). So that the trick will be easily followed by the spectators, be sure to point out which color is on top before you start rolling them. For that matter, it is not even necessary to use bills at all; different-colored slips of paper will work just as well.

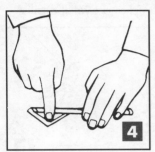

BILLS FROM NOWHERE I

EFFECT

You show your hands to be unmistakably empty. Then, holding your hands together, a quantity of one-dollar bills magically appears from out of your empty palms!

SECRET AND PREPARATION

You must be wearing a suit or sport coat in order to present this effect properly.

A Make a stack of five or six one-dollar bills.

B Roll them into as tight a roll as you can.

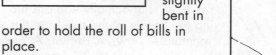

C Place the roll of bills in the crook of your left elbow.

D Pull the fabric of your coat sleeve up and over the bills. Keep your arm slightly bent in order to hold the roll of bills in place.

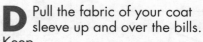

METHOD

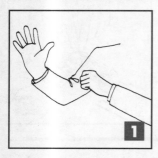

1 With the bills "loaded" as described, face the spectators. Reach over with your left hand and grasp your right coat sleeve at the crook of your elbow. Pull the sleeve back, clear of your right wrist, as you show your right hand is unmistakably empty.

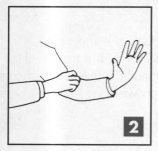

2 Reach across with your right hand and grasp your left coat sleeve at the crook of the elbow and pull that sleeve back and clear of the left wrist, as you show your left hand is empty.

3 During this move, it is very natural for your right fingers to secretly steal the concealed bills from the fold in your jacket.

4 The roll is held in your right hand between your fingers and palm, as shown.

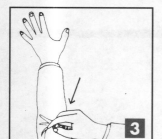

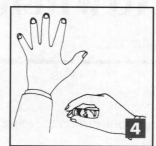

5 Hold both of your hands in front of you at shoulder height, with your left hand in front of your right hand. This position will give you maximum coverage for the next move.

6 Using the thumb and fingers of both hands, unroll the bills so that they begin to appear at the top of your fingers.

7 After unrolling the bills halfway, suddenly pull the left hand down, so that the thumb of your left hand unrolls the bills the rest of the way from the bottom, leaving the open bills in your right hand. Fan the bills and display them to the spectators.

BILLS FROM NOWHERE II

EFFECT

You reach into your pocket and remove your wallet. Opening the wallet, you remove a single one-dollar bill. After replacing the wallet, you clearly demonstrate that, other than the one bill, your hands are absolutely empty. By suddenly slapping the bill against the palm of one hand, the single bill magically multiples into a quantity of new one-dollar bills!

SECRET AND PREPARATION

Place a single bill into a secretarial wallet or checkbook and put the wallet in your inside coat pocket. Prepare a stack of bills as described in Steps A, B, C, and D in BILLS FROM NOWHERE I.

METHOD

1 With the bills loaded into the crook of your left arm, reach into your coat pocket and remove your wallet. Take out the single bill and display it to the spectators. Clearly show your hands to be empty, except for the one bill.

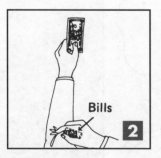

2 With the bill in your left hand, reach over with your right hand and grasp your left coat sleeve at the crook in the elbow. Pull the sleeve back until your left wrist is bare. As you pull back your sleeve, secretly steal the hidden bills with your right hand (as in Step 3 of BILLS FROM NOWHERE I).

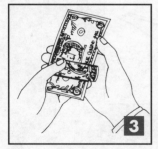

3 With the roll of bills hidden in your right hand, transfer the single bill from your left hand to your right fingers. Place the single bill in front of the roll. The secret roll of bills will be effectively hidden behind the single bill, as shown.

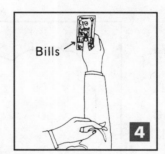

4 Without hesitation, grasp your right sleeve at the crook of the elbow and pull this sleeve back until you bare your right wrist.

NOTE: The spectators will have seen that both of your hands are empty except for the single bill, which has constantly been in view.

5 Behind the visible bill, unroll the hidden bills.

6 As you fan the new bills from behind the single bill, the effect will be the instant multiplication of a single bill into many, an effect sure to captivate any spectator's imagination.

CHAPTER 5

GENIE CARDS

In contrast to tricks with regulation playing cards, Genie tricks require a special type of card. To perform the tricks in this section, you will need to create your own set of Genie cards by copying or tracing the pattern below onto business-card stock and cutting the card out. You will need fifty full-size Genie cards and twenty half-cards.

While several tricks may be performed with the Genie cards, all depend upon the same simple but deceptive move. Although this  move is excellent, you should not perform more than one Genie trick at any performance. It is better to keep a few Genie tricks in reserve, so that for your next show you can switch to another. This keeps people wondering just what to expect, which is an important factor in magic.

If you wish, you can use the Genie cards for an introductory trick, or as an interlude during a program of effects with playing cards, and you will always be on the safe side.

The Genie cards and their routines were specially devised for use with this magic course, which means that they will be entirely new to many people who see them. This gives you a real advantage over the spectators from the start—so make the most of it!

GENIE OF THE LAMP

In this very basic form of the Genie, the only props needed are the cards themselves. The effect is that a Genie mysteriously appears, thanks to the magic of Aladdin's lamp.

EFFECT

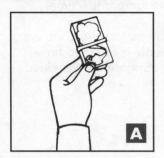

A You show a stack of cards with a rubber band around it. The top card shows a magic lamp giving off a cloud of smoke, but no Genie.

B Remarking that this represents Aladdin's wonderful lamp, you invite a spectator to write their initials in the lamp. You then

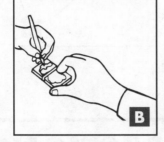

remove the card and state that whenever Aladdin rubbed the lamp, the Genie appeared.

C Holding the card face down in one hand, you rub the lamp with the fingers of your other hand.

D After a few rubs, you turn the card over showing that the Genie has magically appeared in the cloud of smoke, and the spectator's initials are still in the lamp!

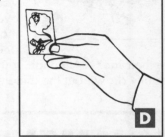

SECRET AND PREPARATION

This basic trick and all the other tricks with the Genie cards depend on a simple, natural movement that secretly switches one card for another. We call this the MASTER MOVE. Here is the explanation of the trick and how the MASTER MOVE makes this a real mystery.

E A special half-card showing only an empty cloud is used, shown here next to the packet of regular full-sized cards. Approximately ten full-sized cards should be used to make up the packet.

F Before the trick, one half-card is placed on the packet so that

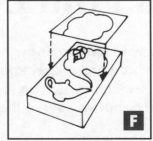

it covers the cloud portion of the top card with the Genie in it.

G You put the rubber band around the cards so that the half-card is held firmly in place, and its bottom edge is completely hidden by the rubber band. Once the half-card is in position and held there by the rubber band, the top card of the packet looks like a full-sized card showing a lamp, a cloud, and nothing else. Use only one half-card when you set up the packet for the trick. Save the others for spares.

METHOD

1 You show the packet to a spectator, and ask the spectator to write their initials in the lamp of the top card.

2 Now for the MASTER MOVE. Holding the packet in your left hand, as shown, you lift up the lamp end of the initialed card with your right finger.

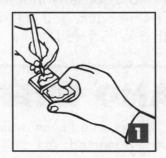

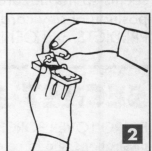

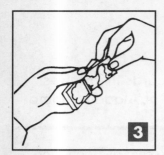

3 Your left hand starts to turn the packet over as you begin to pull out the Genie card with your right fingers.

4 Here is the action as seen from below. The spectators see the back of the packet instead of the face. Everyone is sure you are drawing out the initialed card.

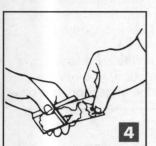

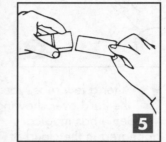

5 As the card comes clear, both the packet and the card have been turned all the way over so that no one can see their faces. Although you have actually drawn out the initialed

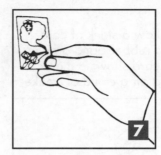

card, the secret half-card remains on the packet. Place the packet face down somewhere out of reach, or drop it in your pocket, so that no one will learn about the half-card.

6 Hold the initialed card face down in your left hand. Place your right fingers under the card and rub the lamp a few times.

7 When you turn the card over, the Genie is found to have magically appeared in the cloud of smoke!

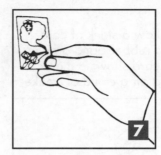

COMMENTS AND SUGGESTIONS

Using the MASTER MOVE, you have secretly switched what the spectators thought was the original Genie card for another; yet the change seems impossible because the person who wrote the initials on the card will find that they are still there. This is something of a miracle in its own right, and when used in association with other effects, it becomes even more sensational. These added details will be covered in the Genie tricks that follow, all using the MASTER MOVE just described.

ROLLOVER FORCE

For some of the Genie card routines, you will need to know how to "force" a playing card, which enables you to know beforehand what card a spectator will select. In other words, the spectator is allowed to make certain "free choices," believing that the end result is out of your control. Here is a very natural force that will serve that purpose perfectly.

The ROLLOVER FORCE is a sure-fire method of forcing a card where the actual handling of the pack seems so haphazard and disorderly that it appears impossible for the magician to have control over the position of any card in the pack. You will need to master ROLLOVER FORCE in order to perform GENIE PREDICTS and GENIE SAVES THE DAY.

SECRET AND PREPARATION

For ROLLOVER FORCE, all you need is an ordinary pack of playing cards with the force card on top. (In the illustrations, the force card is marked with an X.)

MARK WILSON'S GREATEST INSTANT MAGIC TRICKS

METHOD

1 Hold the pack face down, in dealing position, in your left hand. State that you wish to have one card selected from the pack at random. To make sure that this choice is not influenced by you, let the pack itself determine which card will be selected.

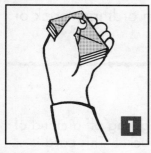

2 With that, you lift the upper ¼ of the pack (about 10 to 15 cards).

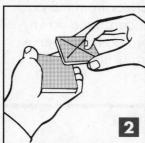

3 Turn these cards over, face up.

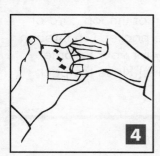

4 As you replace the cards, say, "To completely confuse the order of the pack, I will not only mix the cards, I'll turn some face up and some face down."

5 To make things more confusing, lift off nearly half the deck (20 to 25 cards).

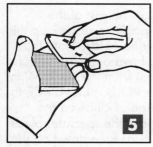

6 Turn these over as before.

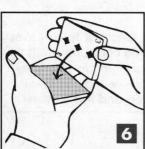

7 Replace these cards on top of the rest of the pack.

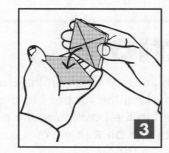

8 To add to all this, lift off another stack of cards, this time cutting closer to the bottom (about ¾ of the deck).

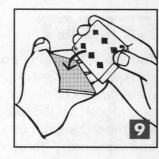

9 Turn these cards over.

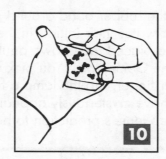

10 Replace them on top of the remaining cards.

11,12,13 You then state, "To confuse matters even further, I'll turn the whole pack over,"—which you do.

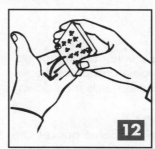

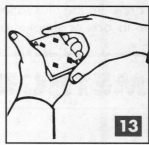

14 After turning the whole pack over, say, "Now we'll run through the pack and take the first face-down card that comes along." With that, you start to spread the pack, "running" the cards from your left hand to your right.

15 The first face-down card you reach will be the force card, the three of clubs. The audience thinks it is just a random card. Have a spectator remove that card from the pack and look at it. When that is done, you have successfully forced the card, using ROLLOVER FORCE.

GENIE PREDICTS

In this Genie trick, you need the pack of Genie cards and an ordinary pack of playing cards, which may be borrowed.

EFFECT

You show the Genie packet with the rubber band around it. The top card shows a magic lamp giving off a cloud of smoke, but no Genie. A spectator writes their initials in the lamp of the top card of the Genie packet. This card is then removed from the packet and placed face down on the table. A card is chosen by the spectator from the pack and placed on the table beside the Genie card. You pick up the Genie card. Keeping the Genie card face down, you reach beneath and, with your finger, rub the lamp a few times. When the card is turned over, both the Genie and the words, "three of clubs," have mysteriously appeared in the cloud. When the chosen card is turned over, it is the three of clubs, proving the Genie's prediction to be correct!

SECRET AND PREPARATION

Before the performance, write the name of any card, say the three of clubs, in the cloud section of the top card of the Genie packet. Cover this top card with the half-card and place the rubber band around the packet. Go through the pack of playing cards, find the three of clubs, and move it to the position in the pack ready for your favorite force. (In the illustrations, the three of clubs has been marked with an X to make it easy to follow.) Place the pack in its box or simply have it lying handy on the table, and you're ready to begin.

METHOD

1 Lay the Genie packet face up on the table and place the pack of playing cards face down beside it.

2 Pick up the Genie packet and point out the empty cloud on the top card, stating, "The Genie, who usually lives in the lamp, apparently isn't home today." Ask a spectator to write their initials in the lamp.

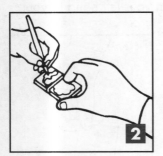

3 Remove the initialed card from the packet (actually the prediction card) using the MASTER MOVE, and place it face down on the table.

4 Put away the rest of the Genie packet and pick up the pack of playing cards. State that you wish to have one card selected at random from the pack. With that, use the ROLLOVER FORCE to force the three of clubs on the spectator. Have the spectator place the chosen card face down on the table next to the Genie card.

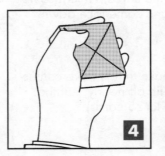

5 Tell the spectator to turn over the Genie card and see if the Genie has anything to say. The spectator will see that the Genie has appeared and has written "three of clubs" in the cloud.

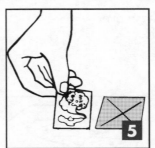

6 When the spectator turns over the playing card, the Genie's prediction proves correct!

COMMENTS AND SUGGESTIONS

In this Genie routine, after you have drawn out the Genie card and placed it on the table, you can let the spectators see the packet of Genie cards face up. Since the half-card is still in place and has no writing in the cloud, it will be mistaken for the second Genie card. Just make sure that the rubber band is still in the proper position, hiding the edge of the half-card. If the half-card has slipped from place, put the packet away without turning it face up. A quick glance will tell you what to do. Also, if you use a pencil to write the Genie's prediction, you can later erase it and use the Genie card over again.

GENIE SAVES THE DAY

EFFECT

In this Genie card effect, you make a prediction, writing it in the Genie's cloud. When the prediction goes wrong, the Genie magically fixes it, producing a double surprise. Again, the MASTER MOVE is used along with the ROLLOVER FORCE of a card from a regular pack of playing cards.

SECRET AND PREPARATION

To prepare, write the name of a playing card, say the three of clubs, in the cloud section of the top Genie card. Cover this with one of the blank half-cards and place the rubber band around the packet. From an ordinary pack of cards, remove the three of clubs and place it at the correct position in the pack, ready for the ROLLOVER FORCE.

METHOD

1 State that you are going to make a prediction—you will predict the very same card that a spectator will later select from an ordinary deck of playing cards! Openly write the name of some other card, say the five of hearts, in the Genie's cloud, stating that this is your prediction.

2 Actually, your prediction is written on the half-card that no one knows about. You have the spectator put their initials in the lamp to identify the prediction card.

3 Go through the MASTER MOVE, laying the Genie card (actually the three of clubs prediction card) face down on the table and place a coin or other small object on top of it. The half-card with your five-of-hearts prediction remains on the Genie packet.

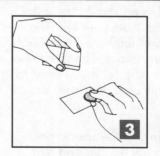

NOTE: Placing a coin or other small object on the Genie card is important, as it discourages anyone from turning the card over until you're ready.

4 Drop the Genie packet in your pocket and bring out the pack of playing cards. Remove the pack from its box and force the three of clubs on the spectator using the ROLLOVER FORCE.

5 Ask the spectator to look at the selected card and see if your prediction is correct. The spectator sees that you are wrong, since the spectator saw you write "five of hearts" on the Genie card, and the card the spectator selected is the three of clubs.

6 That's when you call on the invisible Genie for help. Remove the coin and ask the spectator to turn over the prediction card. The spectator will find that the Genie has magically appeared and has changed your prediction to the three of clubs, the same card the spectator selected. Hooray for the Genie!

COMMENTS AND SUGGESTIONS

This effect is super for three reasons. One, it fulfills a prediction; two, it mysteriously changes one prediction into another; and three, it proves you are right when the spectator thinks that you are wrong. The combination will have your spectators trying to figure out three things at once, which is sure to leave them totally baffled.

One word of caution. You must keep the packet of Genie cards face down after the MASTER MOVE, so that no one will see the false prediction on the half-card. Just drop the packet in your pocket and you will find that by the end of the trick, the spectators will have forgotten about the packet completely.

ROLL ANY NUMBER

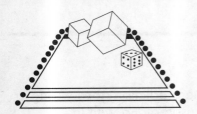

The following force illustrates how you can cleverly manipulate a spectator, without anyone catching on.

METHOD

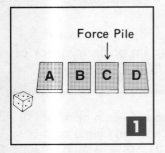

1 This force uses a single die from any pair of dice. It will work with any four objects. To aid in the explanation, we will assume that the object to be forced is one of four piles in a single row. The pile to be forced should be in the third position from your left. The four piles are numbered A through D in the illustrations. The pile to be forced is the C pile. If you want to force a single card, that card should be on top of the "force" pile.

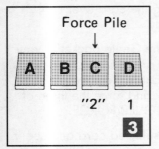

2 Explain that the spectator should roll the die and that you will count its number along the row in order to choose a pile.

3 If the roll is two, begin counting from the right to the left. Your count will end on the desired pile.

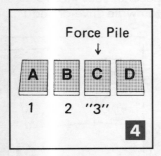

4 If the roll is three, begin counting from left to right to reach the correct pile.

5 If the spectator rolls a five, count from left to right. When you reach the end of the row on four, continue the count, back from right to left, to land on the proper pile (C).

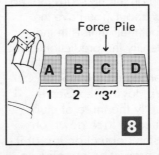

NOTE: Do not count pile D as five, just immediately start your count back from four on pile D to five on pile C, your force pile.

6 If the roll is six, count from right to left and then return to the right to finish the count.

NOTE: In this case, you do count pile D as four. Then just continue as if starting from the right, counting pile D as five and pile C as six.

7 The force will not work with rolls of one or four, but such rolls make it all the better, as they allow you to inject a clever twist that adds to the effect. If a one or a four turns up on the die, immediately say, "Good! We will use the 'hidden number,' the one that nobody knows!"

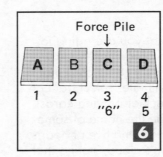

8 With that, pick up the die, turn it over, and point to the bottom number, referring to this as the hidden number. If one is rolled, the hidden number will be six. If four is rolled, the hidden number will be three. In either case, you end up with a number that enables you to count to the required pile. Tell the spectator to look at the top card of the pile, and you're done!

GENIE'S NUMBER

In this trick, the Genie does magical mathematics and predicts a chosen number. The Genie does it very well, as you will see.

SECRET AND PREPARATION

A Before the trick, write the number 1089 in the cloud at the top Genie card.

B Cover it with the empty half-card and place a rubber band around the packet.

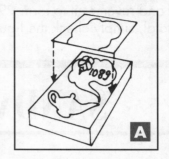

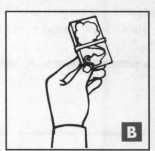

METHOD

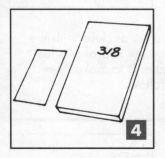

1 Have a spectator write their initials in the lamp, as you did in GENIE OF THE LAMP.

2 Remove the initialed card using the MASTER MOVE (actually removing the card with 1089 written on it) and place it face down on the table.

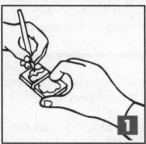

3 Lay a pad and pencil beside it.

4 Tell the spectator, "I want you to write a number that uses three different figures, any number between 100 and 1,000, without letting me see it." Let's say that the spectator writes 318.

5 You continue, "Reverse that number and subtract the smaller number from the larger."

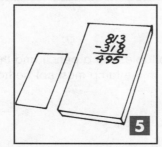

NOTE: Here you tell the spectator that if the answer is less than 100 to leave a zero in front of it so the number will still have three figures.

6 As soon as the spectator has done the subtraction, you state, "Reverse your answer and write it just below." When the spectator does this, say, "I want you to add those two numbers so you will get a grand total."

7 Tell the spectator to circle the grand total and lay the pad down beside the Genie card.

8 Explain that you will call on your invisible Genie to check the spectator's arithmetic. Pick up the Genie card and place it face down on top of the pad. Pretend to catch the Genie out of the air and slip the Genie between the pad and Genie card.

9 After a few moments, ask the spectator to turn over the card. To the amazement of the spectator, the Genie has appeared showing the same number as their slip, 1089.

COMMENTS AND SUGGESTIONS

Whatever the original three-figure number, the grand total will always be 1089, unless the original figures are all alike, as 333 or 555. That is why you tell the spectator to write a number with three different figures. When subtracted, they will always produce numbers that, when reversed and added, will total 1089. In some cases, such as 463 minus 364, the subtraction yields 99. That is why you tell the spectator to put a zero in front of anything under 100, so if the spectator makes it 099 and reverses it to form 990, the two numbers will add up to the usual 1089. If the spectator should get some other total, simply check the figures and the spectator will find that the Genie was right all along!

SANDWICHED GENIE

EFFECT

This is similar to GENIE PREDICTS. In this trick, after the spectator has initialed the lamp, the spectator places the Genie card in the center of a deck of playing cards. When the deck is spread, the spectator finds that the Genie has not only mysteriously appeared, but the Genie has also magically written the names of two playing cards in the cloud of smoke. Upon inspection, the spectator finds that these are the two playing cards that are next to the Genie card in the deck!

SECRET AND PREPARATION

In addition to the Genie cards, you will need a regular deck of playing cards.

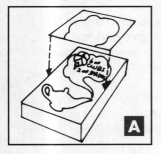

A Before you perform the trick, use a pencil to write the names of any two playing cards in the cloud of smoke on the top card of the Genie card packet. Let's suppose that you write the six of clubs and the two of spades. This is now your Genie prediction card.

B Cover your prediction card with one of the empty-cloud half-cards and put the rubber band around the packet. From the deck of playing cards, remove the two of spades and the six of clubs.

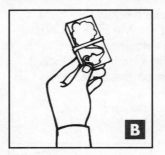

C Put the six of clubs on the top of the deck of playing cards.

D Put the two of spades on the bottom of the deck of playing cards and place the deck back in the box. You are ready to perform the trick.

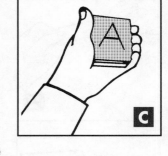

NOTE: In the illustrations, we have marked the six of clubs with the letter A and the two of spades with the letter B to make them easier to follow.

METHOD

1 To begin the presentation, lay the Genie packet face up on the table with a pencil and the box of playing cards. Remark that the Genie who usually lives in the lamp must not be home. Ask a spectator to write their initials in the lamp of the top card.

2 Remove the initialed card using the MASTER MOVE (actually removing the prediction card) and lay it face down on the table. Put the rest of the Genie cards in your pocket or just lay them aside.

3 Tell the spectator to write their name on the back of the Genie card. While the spectator is writing, pick up the deck of playing cards, remove it from the box and set it on the table next to the Genie card.

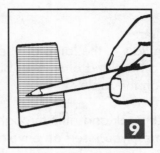

4 Ask the spectator to divide the deck into two parts. Tell the spectator to cut anywhere in the deck and to place the upper portion on the table on the other side of the Genie card.

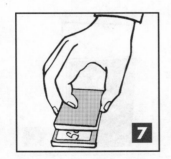

5 Stress the fact that the spectator is the one who is deciding where to cut the pack.

6 Tell the spectator to place the Genie card face down on top of this new pile (which places it on top of the six of clubs).

7 Tell the spectator to place the lower half of the deck on top of the Genie card, thus burying it in the deck. (This now places the two of spades, which was on the bottom of the deck, directly above the Genie card.)

NOTE: At this point, the Genie card has been "sandwiched" between the six of clubs and the two of spades, while the spectators think the Genie card was placed in the deck at a freely chosen spot.

8 State that you will have to call on the Genie to help with this trick. Explaining that the Genie is always invisible when not at home, pretend to spot the Genie in the air. Reach out and "catch" the Genie in your hand. Pretend to slip the Genie into the pack of cards on the table.

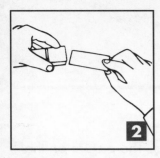

9 Pick up the pencil, lay it on the end of the pack, and say, "This Genie is very intelligent. With a pencil, this Genie can even write." Move the pencil forward, sliding it completely across the top of the pack. Lay the pencil aside.

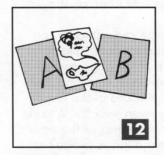

10 Say, "That gave the Genie time to write a message. Let's see if that happened." With that, you spread the pack along the table.

11 Push the Genie card out of the deck along with the card just below it (A) and the card just above it (B), as shown.

12 Say, "I'll just turn over the Genie card, and we'll see what the Genie knows." When the signed Genie card is turned over, the names of the two playing cards are seen in the cloud with the spectator's initials still in the lamp.

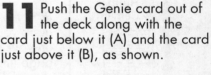

13 Turn over cards A and B, showing the six of clubs and the two of spades, amazing the spectators.

COMMENTS AND SUGGESTIONS

As in the previous trick, once you have drawn out the previously prepared Genie prediction card, you may allow the spectators to see the face of the packet of Genie cards. As long as the half-card is still in place and securely bound by the rubber band, they will think they are seeing the second Genie card in the packet. Be sure to glance at the face of the packet, though, to be sure that the rubber band is still hiding the edge of the half-card.

GENIE'S LIBRARY

EFFECT

You have a spectator write their initials in the lamp on the face card of a packet of Genie cards. The picture on the card shows a magic lamp giving off a cloud of smoke, but no Genie. You remove the initialed Genie card from the stack and place it face down on the table.

You display an ordinary paperback book and riffle through its pages, inviting the spectator to call "Stop" at any time during the riffle. When the call comes, you insert an envelope in the book to mark the exact page selected by the spectator. The spectator is then asked to note the word in the text located in the upper right corner of the selected page.

In an attempt to locate the Genie and learn the selected word, the Genie card is partially inserted into the book for only a brief moment. When the card is removed and turned face up, it shows that both the Genie and the exact word that was selected from the text have magically appeared—with the word written in the Genie's cloud of smoke!

SECRET AND PREPARATION

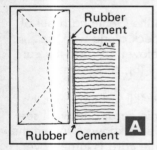

A Carefully cut one page from the center of the paperback book you plan to use and place it on your table, with the front of the page (that is, the odd-numbered side of the page that was originally facing the front of the book) facing up. Apply a very thin strip of rubber cement along the binding edge of the page and on the top edge of the envelope, as shown.

B Allow the cement to dry on both surfaces and attach the glued edge of the page to the glued edge of the envelope. Be sure that the edges of the page are exactly even with the left side and the lower edges of the envelope. Although this is difficult to describe in written form, it is really quite simple to make. Just study the pictures and you will see exactly how to make this special envelope prop that is the key to the entire trick.

NOTE: The envelope should be longer and wider than the book page, so that when it is turned over, the page will be completely hidden from view beneath the envelope.

C After the glue has set, insert the prepared envelope into the book so that the secret page is lined up with the rest of the pages in the book. If this is done correctly, everything should appear natural from all angles. It will look like a book with an envelope stuck in its pages.

D Write the prediction word from the force page (the page you have glued to the envelope) in the cloud of the top card of the Genie packet. Cover this with the half-card and place the rubber band around the entire stack.

METHOD

1 Place the packet of Genie cards on the table and bring the book into view, casually showing it on both sides. Turn the book face up and remove the envelope with your right hand. Make sure not to flash the attached page as you do this.

2 Pick up and display the packet of Genie cards. Have a spectator write their initials in the lamp of the top Genie card as usual. Remove the initialed card using the MASTER MOVE (actually removing the prediction card). Place the card face down on the table.

3 Pick up the book in your left hand and riffle through the pages with your left thumb. Ask the spectator to call "Stop" at any time during the riffle.

4 When the call comes, stop riffling.

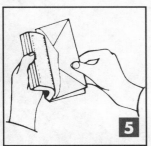

5 Insert the envelope into the book at that point. Be sure the bottom of the envelope is lined up evenly with the bottom

edge of the book. Also, insert the envelope all the way into the book so that the glued edge of the envelope and the secret prediction page are wedged securely into the binding of the book.

6 Without hesitation, gently tap the bottom edge of the book on the table. This squares up the envelope (and the hidden page) with the rest of the pages of the book.

7 Immediately lay the book on the table and pick up the initialed Genie card.

NOTE: Picking up the Genie card at this time is actually a clever ruse to let you set down the book with the special envelope inserted into it. If you did not use the Genie card here, there would be no reason for you not to show the spectator the page that was selected.

8 Slide the Genie card face down through the pages of the book. Say, "I will now attempt to locate the magic Genie within the pages of this book, where the Genie frequently visits on vacation. If we're lucky, perhaps the

Genie will also reveal to us the word that you selected." After this bit of banter, replace the prediction card face down on the table.

9 Here is the most important move in the trick. Pick up the book and open it.

10 The book should hinge open between the envelope and the secretly attached page. The envelope should cover the left-hand portion of the book, exposing the front side of the attached force page. Point out to the spectator the last word in the top line of this page (actually the force word). Ask the spectator to remember that word.

Force Page

NOTE: Do not look at the page or the word as you do this. Hold the book away from you so that it faces the spectator and you obviously cannot see the freely selected page. Unknown to the spectator, you have now forced the spectator to choose a word that appears to be the result of random selection.

11 Close the book and remove the envelope, bringing along the secret page. Immediately place the envelope aside, or better yet, into your coat pocket, making sure not to expose the secret page as you do.

12 To bring the mystery to its close, ask the spectator to call out the selected word. When the spectator does, turn over the Genie card, revealing both the Genie and the word written in the cloud that exactly matches the word selected from the text of the book!

COMMENTS AND SUGGESTIONS

Be sure to use a book that does not open out flat for this trick. A paperback book is best. If the book opens wide, the spectators might notice that the page the volunteer freely selected is actually glued to the envelope.

Do not call any unnecessary attention to the envelope during the presentation. Handle it as if its only purpose is to mark the selected page in the book. After it has done its work, place it in your pocket and continue. By the end of the trick, the spectators will most likely forget that you ever used any additional prop other than the book.

SPECIAL NOTE: Since all of the Genie tricks use the same magical principles, the half-card and the MASTER MOVE, you should present only one of the Genie tricks at any one performance. Never repeat a trick for the same spectators.

CHAPTER 6

SILK AND HANDKERCHIEF MAGIC

Accomplished magicians are able to perform magic anywhere they happen to be. And many people, including magic experts and historians, consider magic with *ordinary objects* to be the strongest and most baffling form of our art. That's one of the reasons why tricks with silks and handkerchiefs are so popular: Everyone either carries a handkerchief themselves or knows somebody who does.

Handkerchiefs come in a great variety of sizes, shapes, colors, and designs and are made from many different types of material. The type of handkerchief to be used in certain tricks is determined by the desired effect. Larger handkerchiefs are better for effects involving knots. Handkerchiefs with patterns, such as a bandanna, aid concealment of small objects in the folds. For effects where the handkerchief seems unimportant, a plain white handkerchief is best. At times, you may borrow such handkerchiefs. Then if you happen to bring out one of your own, nobody will suspect trickery.

Some magicians use colored silk handkerchiefs, or "silks." Silks are made from thin silk and have a very narrow hem, making them compressible. Large silks with colorful ornamental designs are excellent for elaborate effects. For less elaborate effects, such as bare-hand productions, vanishes, color changes, and the like, small silks are preferable.

Whatever the choice, the Instant Magic silk-and-handkerchief tricks in this section will have an even stronger effect on the spectators when performed with finesse and expertise.

HYPNOTIZED HANDKERCHIEF

EFFECT

You display a pocket handkerchief and twirl it between your hands in a rope-like fashion. Always under your control, the handkerchief stands erect, bows to the spectators, and moves back and forth in a very puzzling manner. You then attach an "invisible" thread to the upper corner of the handkerchief and cause the handkerchief to follow your lead by pulling on the magical leash. Even after crushing the handkerchief down with your other hand, you cannot seem to discourage the persistent performance of the HYPNOTIZED HANDKERCHIEF.

METHOD

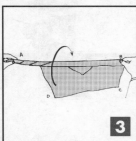

1 Borrow a spectator's handkerchief (or use your own) and spread it open on the table. Hold the left-hand corner (A) between your left thumb and fingers and grasp the hem at the center of the right side (B) with your right hand, as shown.

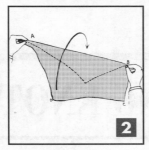

2, 3 Pick up the handkerchief and hold it in front of you. Twirl the handkerchief between your hands.

4 Continue twirling until the entire handkerchief is rolled in a tightly twisted, rope-like configuration.

5 As you continue to hold the twisted handkerchief, move your right hand above your left, so that the right end (B) is directly above the left end (A), as shown.

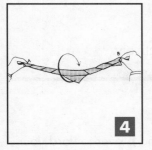

6 Move your left hand up, so that it can grasp the rolled handkerchief near the center. Do not allow the twists in the handkerchief to unroll as you change the position of your left hand. Your right hand maintains its grip on the top end (B).

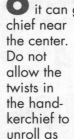

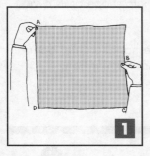

7 Pull the handkerchief tight between your hands. Then, slowly release the handkerchief from your right fingers. It will stand erect, as if hypnotized. (In reality, the natural rigidity given to the material by the many twists is what causes the handkerchief to maintain its upright position.)

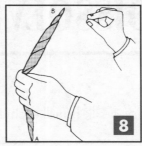

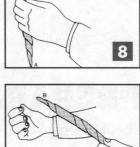

8 Pretend to pluck an imaginary strand of hair from your head and go through the motion of tying it to the upper end of the handkerchief (B). Holding the free end of this fictitious hair in your hand, slowly pull it toward your body. At the same time, draw your left thumb gently downward against your left fingers. The downward motion of your thumb will cause the handkerchief to obediently lean in your direction.

NOTE: Practice will teach you how to synchronize the handkerchief's leaning movement with the pulling motion of the "invisible" hair in your right hand.

9 Move your right hand and the "invisible" hair forward, toward the spectators. To make the handkerchief lean away from you and follow the "invisible" tug, simply slide your left thumb up and forward on the center of the handkerchief.

10 Here is a more detailed illustration of the move required for Step 8. This shows how the left thumb pulls down on the center of the handkerchief to make it lean toward you.

11 Here is the action, as your left thumb pushes up and forward on the center of the handkerchief, causing the handkerchief to lean away from you for Step 9.

12 After repeating this back and forth pulling movement with the "invisible" hair several times, bring the handkerchief back to its original upright position. Hold your right hand above the hypnotized handkerchief, as shown.

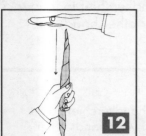

13 In one swift downward motion, bring your right hand down on top of the handkerchief,

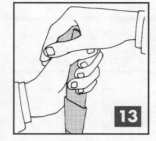

crushing it between your right palm and the top of your left fist.

14 Quickly raise your right hand back up. As you do, secretly use your right fingers and thumb to straighten the handkerchief.

15 Bring the handkerchief back to its original, hypnotized, upright position. With practice, you will learn to execute this upward movement so swiftly and smoothly that the handkerchief will appear to bounce back into shape of its own accord.

16 To conclude the effect, snap the handkerchief open and offer it to the spectators for examination.

DISSOLVING KNOT

EFFECT

You casually tie a knot in the center of a silk handkerchief. Then the knot simply "melts" away.

SECRET AND PREPARATION

You will need a handkerchief (silk is best) at least 18" square, in order to present this trick effectively.

METHOD

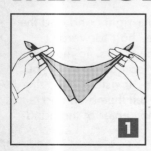

1 Grasp the diagonal corners of the handkerchief between the first and second fingers of each hand.

2 Twirl the handkerchief into a loose, rope-like configuration. We will call the end pinched between the first and second fingers of your left hand End A and the end in your right hand End B.

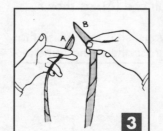

3 Bring End B over toward your left and open the second and third fingers of your left hand, as shown.

4 Lay End B over End A, passing end B between the second and third fingers of your left hand.

5 Your right hand reaches through the loop and grasps End A, as shown. The third and fourth fingers of your left hand curl around the twisted silk below End A.

6 After the third and fourth fingers of the left hand are closed around the handkerchief, the second finger of your left hand hooks the silk just below where the two ends cross, below End B, as shown.

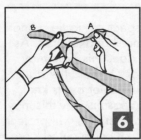

7 This is the key move. Pull End A through the loop with your right hand. End B is held firmly by the thumb and first finger of your left hand. The third and fourth fingers of your left hand release their grip around the silk, as your left second finger hooks and pulls the lower portion of End B through the loop. Study the illustration carefully.

8 As you continue pulling on End A, a knot will form around the loop held by

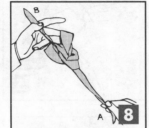

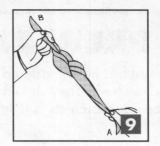

the second finger of your left hand, as shown. When this knot is tight enough to hold its shape, remove your left second finger from inside the loop.

9 You now have apparently tied a real knot in the handkerchief. Really you have cleverly (and secretly) tied a slip knot. If you were to pull on the ends of the handkerchief now, the knot would dissolve.

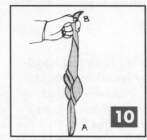

10 Allow the handkerchief to hang freely from the thumb and first finger of your left hand.

11 Grasp End A lightly with the thumb and first finger of your right hand. Hold the handkerchief horizontally in front of you and gently blow on the knot. At that same time, pull on the ends of the handkerchief and the knot will dissolve away!

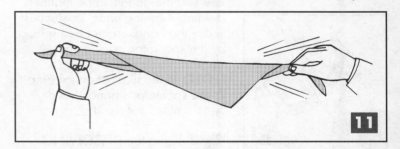

COMMENTS AND SUGGESTIONS

The DISSOLVING KNOT is one of the basic, classic effects in magic. It is important that you practice until you can tie the DISSOLVING KNOT just as easily and quickly as you would a real knot. The ability to tie this trick knot will then become the basis for many other baffling effects.

HANDKERCHIEF THROUGH HANDKERCHIEF

EFFECT

You display two silk handkerchiefs. You twist one into a rope-like configuration and give it to a spectator to hold outstretched between the spectator's hands. You then twist the second handkerchief in the same manner and tie it around the first handkerchief held by the spectator. The spectator is asked to tie a knot in the handkerchief so that both handkerchiefs are securely bonded together. Under these impossible conditions, you cause the handkerchiefs to melt apart, leaving their knots intact.

SECRET AND PREPARATION

In order to perform this trick, you must first have mastered the DISSOLVING KNOT.
You will require two large silk handkerchiefs. They should be at least 18" square and preferably of contrasting colors. In the illustrations, one of the handkerchiefs is light in color, and the other is dark. This makes the description easier to follow.

METHOD

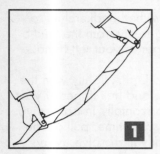

1 Grasp the light-colored handkerchief by two diagonal corners and twirl it between your hands into a loose rope. Hand it to a spectator and require that the spectator hold it outstretched by those same corners, as shown.

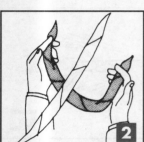

2 Twirl the dark-colored handkerchief in the same manner. Holding it by the ends, position it under the handkerchief being held by the spectator, as shown.

NOTE: In the illustration for Step 2, the spectator's hands have been omitted for clarity.

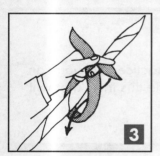

3 Utilizing the DISSOLVING KNOT, tie the dark handkerchief around the light handkerchief.

4 With the fake knot cinched up tightly against the light-colored handkerchief, loop the dark handkerchief around the light handkerchief a second time and tie one legitimate knot.

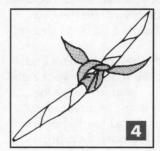

5 Ask the spectator to tie a knot in the other handkerchief. As the spectator does this, you may find it necessary to hold the dark-colored handkerchief by its knot. There are two reasons why this may be necessary. First, this will protect the fake knot from being pulled loose. Second, this prevents the spectator from tying the knot too tightly around your handkerchief. You can avoid this possibility by tying both knots yourself, but the effectiveness of the illusion is enhanced if the spectator ties the real knot in the light-colored handkerchief.

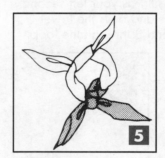

6 Have the spectator hold the corners of the light handkerchief, as you hold the corners of the dark handkerchief. With a gentle shaking motion, pull on the ends of your handkerchief and instruct the spectator to do the same. Your knot will dissolve, and the two handkerchiefs will magically separate from each other. Because of the second real knot that you tied and the real knot that the spectator tied, you are both left with knots in your handkerchiefs! Done correctly, this is a beautiful and baffling mystery.

PENETRATING HANDKERCHIEF

Here is a simple but effective mystery involving objects easily found around the house. All you need is an ordinary drinking glass, two handkerchiefs, and a rubber band. This is another of those little gems from the inventive mind of "Gen" Grant.

MARK WILSON'S GREATEST INSTANT MAGIC TRICKS

EFFECT

You display a drinking glass, holding it mouth up with the tips of your fingers. You place a handkerchief in the glass and cover both the handkerchief and the glass with a second handkerchief. Next, you place a rubber band over the second handkerchief and the glass, thus sealing the first handkerchief inside the glass. Holding the glass from the outside, you reach under the handkerchief for a brief moment and instantly withdraw the first handkerchief—the one that was sealed inside the glass! The outside handkerchief is removed and all may now be examined. An impossible penetration!

SECRET AND PREPARATION

This trick depends entirely upon a simple move that involves secretly turning the glass upside down while it is being covered by the second handkerchief. All of the illustrations are from your point of view.

METHOD

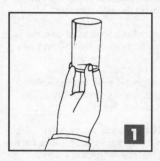

1 Begin by holding the drinking glass, mouth up, with the tips of the fingers and thumb of your right hand, as shown.

2 Display a handkerchief. With your left hand, push it into the glass. (This is the handkerchief that will later penetrate the glass.)

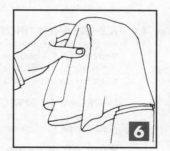

3 Pick up the second handkerchief with your left hand. Bring it up in front of the glass, momentarily hiding the glass from the spectators' view.

4 Here comes the secret move. As you begin to cover the glass with the handkerchief, your right hand slightly relaxes its grip on the bottom of the glass, allowing the glass to pivot between your thumb and fingers.

5 Let the glass pivot until it has turned completely upside down.

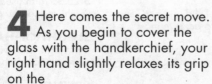

NOTE: The handkerchief inside the glass should be large enough so that it will not fall out when you turn the glass upside down.

6 As the glass turns over, your left hand finishes covering both your right hand and the glass.

7 After the glass is covered, grip the glass through the cloth with your left hand, as shown.

8 Remove your right hand, casually showing it empty, and pick up the rubber band from the table. Spread the rubber band with your right fingers and place it around the handkerchief and the top of the glass. (Unknown to the spectators, it is really the bottom!)

9 With your right hand, reach underneath the covering handkerchief and grasp the first handkerchief—the one that is inside the glass. Pull it straight down into view. To the spectators, it appears that the handkerchief has magically penetrated the bottom of the glass!

10 With your right hand, reach under the covering handkerchief and grip the glass in position to make the secret pivot once again, this time with the mouth of the glass (which is at the bottom because the glass is upside down) between the tips of your right thumb and fingers.

11 With your left hand, grip the outer (second) handkerchief between the tips of the fingers at the very "top" of the covered glass (actually the real bottom) and pull the cloth just enough to release the rubber band from around the glass, and then stop. Pause for a moment, just long enough to allow the glass to pivot in the fingers back to its original mouth-up position.

12 As soon as the glass is mouth up, draw the handkerchief away from the glass, and all can be examined.

GLOSSARY

BETCHA: A classification of "magical puzzles" in which the magician "bets" a spectator that they cannot duplicate a stunt or trick about to be performed.

CLASSIC-PALM POSITION: Method of hiding a small object by gently squeezing it in the palm of your hand.

CLOSE-UP TRICK: Any trick that can be performed at close quarters to an audience. Card and coin tricks, among others, are generally referred to as Close-Up tricks.

COIN FOLD: Method of folding a coin in a piece of paper, yet being able to secretly remove it without the spectators' knowledge.

COIN ROLL: Classic manipulation of a coin rolling across the back of a performer's hand.

COINS ACROSS: Close-Up routine in which two or more coins apparently move from one place to another.

EFFECT: Description of how a magic trick looks to an audience.

FINGER-PALM POSITION: One of the many methods of concealing a coin or other small object by holding it with the fingers and keeping the hand in a natural position.

FORCE PILE: A stack of playing cards that contains one or more cards the magician wishes to force.

FREE CHOICE: Legitimately free selection of a playing card from a deck.

FRENCH DROP: Classic coin manipulation in which a coin is apparently placed into the hand yet vanishes.

GENIE CARD: Specially printed card, about the size of a business card, used to perform many special Close-Up tricks. The card depicts a Genie rising in a wisp of smoke from a lamp. (See page 70.)

HALF-CARD: The basic secret to all Genie Card routines. The Half-Card, which depicts the top part of the Genie drawing, is placed on top of a packet of full-sized Genie Cards, and held in place with a rubber band.

ICE-BREAKER TRICKS: Very simple, basic, yet clever tricks, the secrets of which may be shared with the audience as a way of establishing a rapport with them. Ice-Breaker tricks are often expendable tricks.

IMPROMPTU EFFECT: Effects that are done on the spur of the moment, without advance preparation, and generally with everyday objects.

INDICATOR CARD: A playing card used to identify the location, value, or suit of a different card, usually selected by the audience. Also called a Key Card.

INSTANT MAGIC: Magic tricks, "Betchas," and other stunts that can apparently be performed on the spur of the moment.

KEY CARD: Any card that can be used as a locator card.

LAPPING: The act of apparently picking an object off a table, yet secretly allowing it to drop into your lap.

MASTER MOVE: Method of sliding one Genie Card from a packet in order to achieve most Genie Card routines.

METHOD: Description of how a magic trick works.

MISDIRECTION: Distracting the audience's attention from one place to another during crucial portions of the magic presentation.

PALM: General term used to describe hiding small objects in the hand. There are several subcategories and types of palms.

PATTER THEME: The basis for any story, real or imaginary, used during the performance of magic.

PENETRATION: One of the many subcategories of magic tricks, specifically, the apparent ability to pass one solid object through another.

RELEASE: The magical separation of one or more items that seem hopelessly intertwined or bound together.

ROLL DOWN: Advanced coin manipulation in which a stack of coins is single-handedly spread between the fingers of one hand.

ROLLOVER FORCE: One of many card-forcing methods in which a spectator thinks they have a free choice, yet the magician knows beforehand which card will be selected.

ROUTINING: Combining two or more individual tricks into a "flowing" performance pattern. For example, a rope routine may be a five-minute act made up of six or seven individual rope tricks, yet the tricks flow smoothly from one to another.

SANDWICHED CARD: Any card that is placed, or located, between two other pre-designated cards.

SELF-WORKING TRICK: Any trick that can be performed with little, if any, secret "moves" or sleight-of-hand maneuvers.

SILKS: Term used to describe colorful silk handkerchiefs used by professional magicians.

SLEIGHT-OF-HAND: General term describing any magic trick whose method relies on skilled manipulation of the fingers and/or hand.

SPRING: Describes action of objects as they are rapidly passed from one hand to another. Usually used in connection with playing-card manipulations.

STUNT: A simple magic trick or "Betcha," usually performed tongue-in-cheek with a lot of humor.

TRICK: General definition for all types of individual magic.